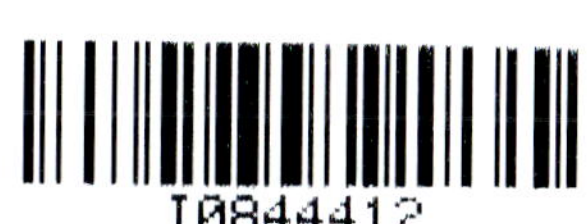

This coloring book belongs to:

....

....

....

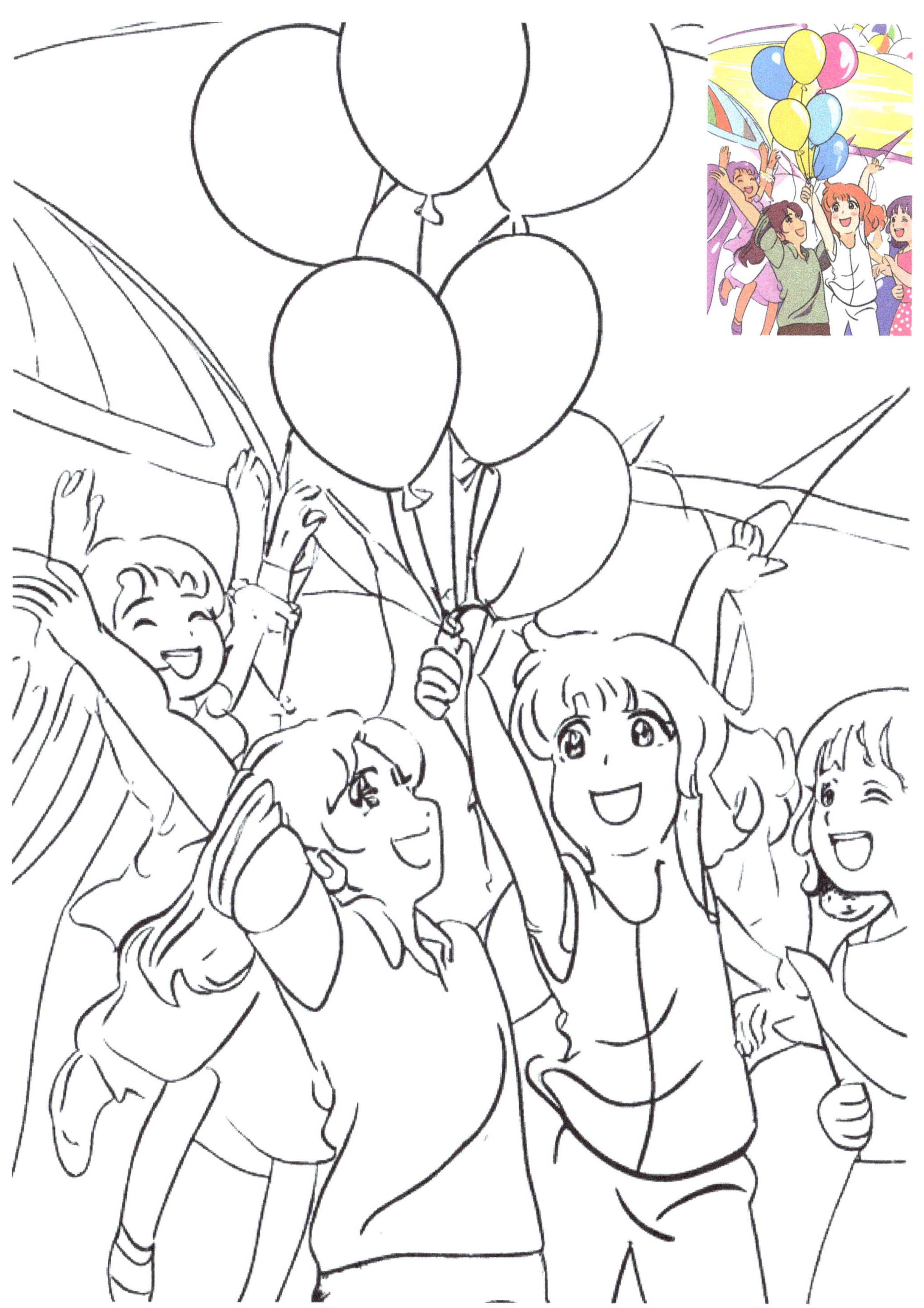

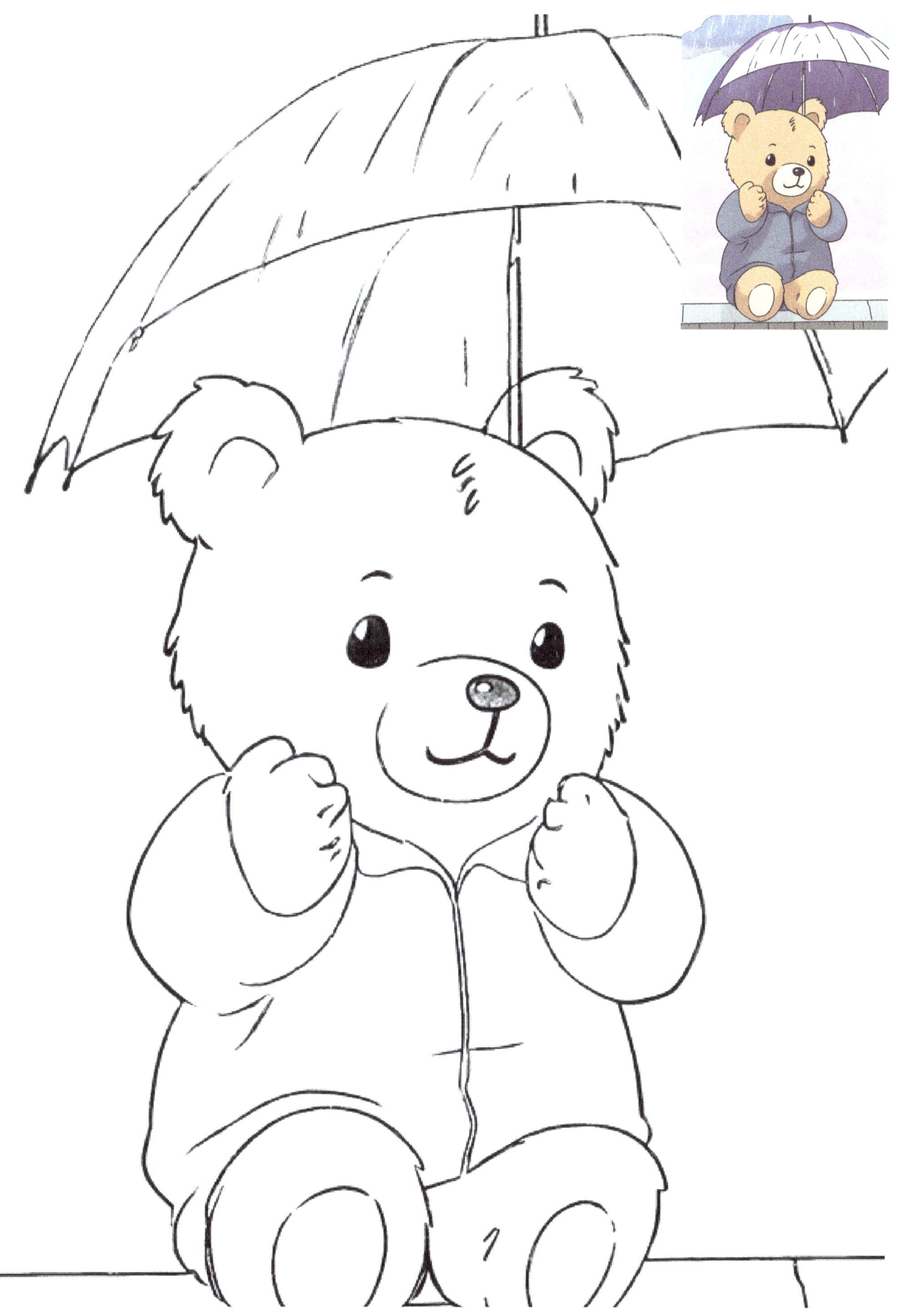

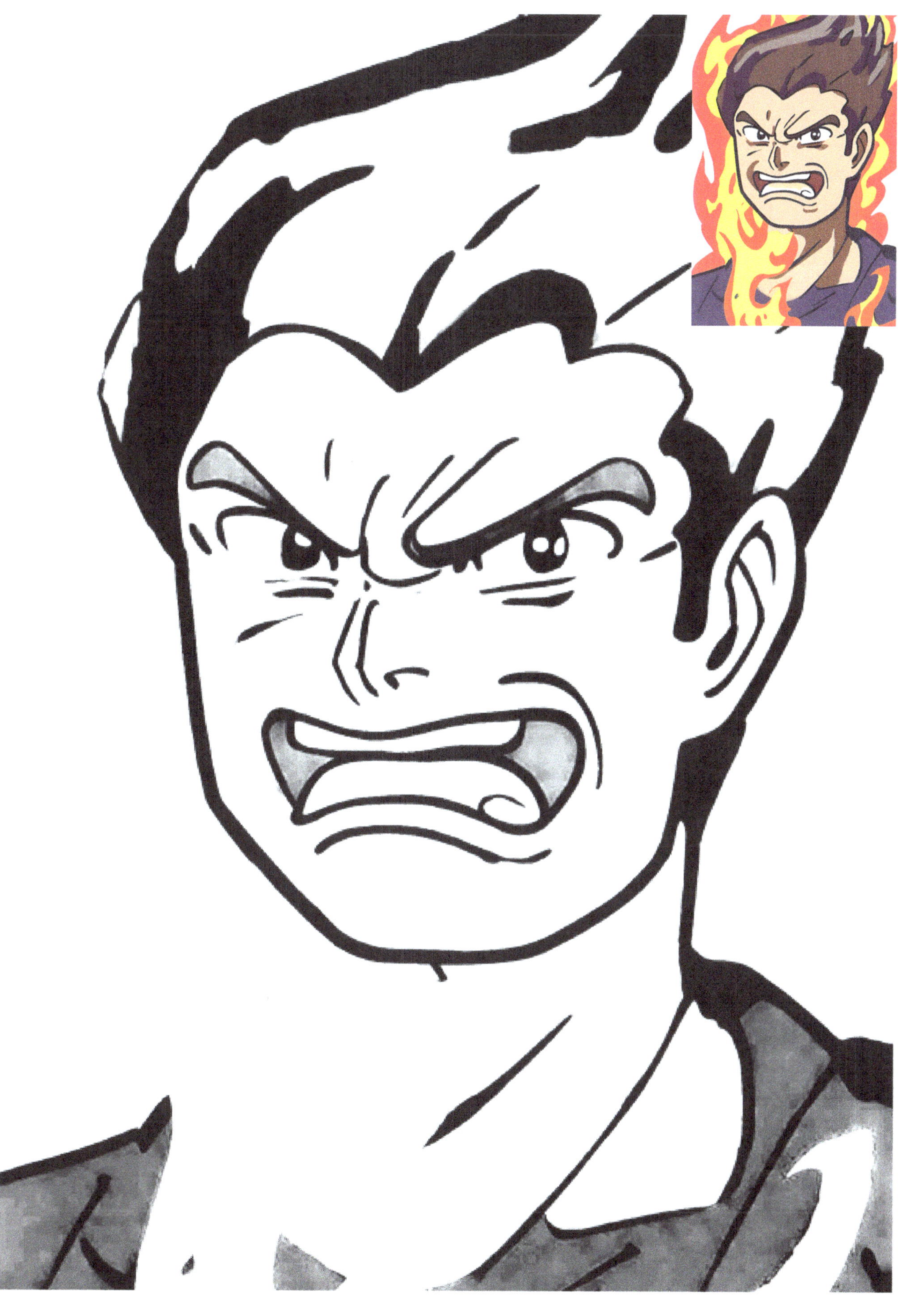

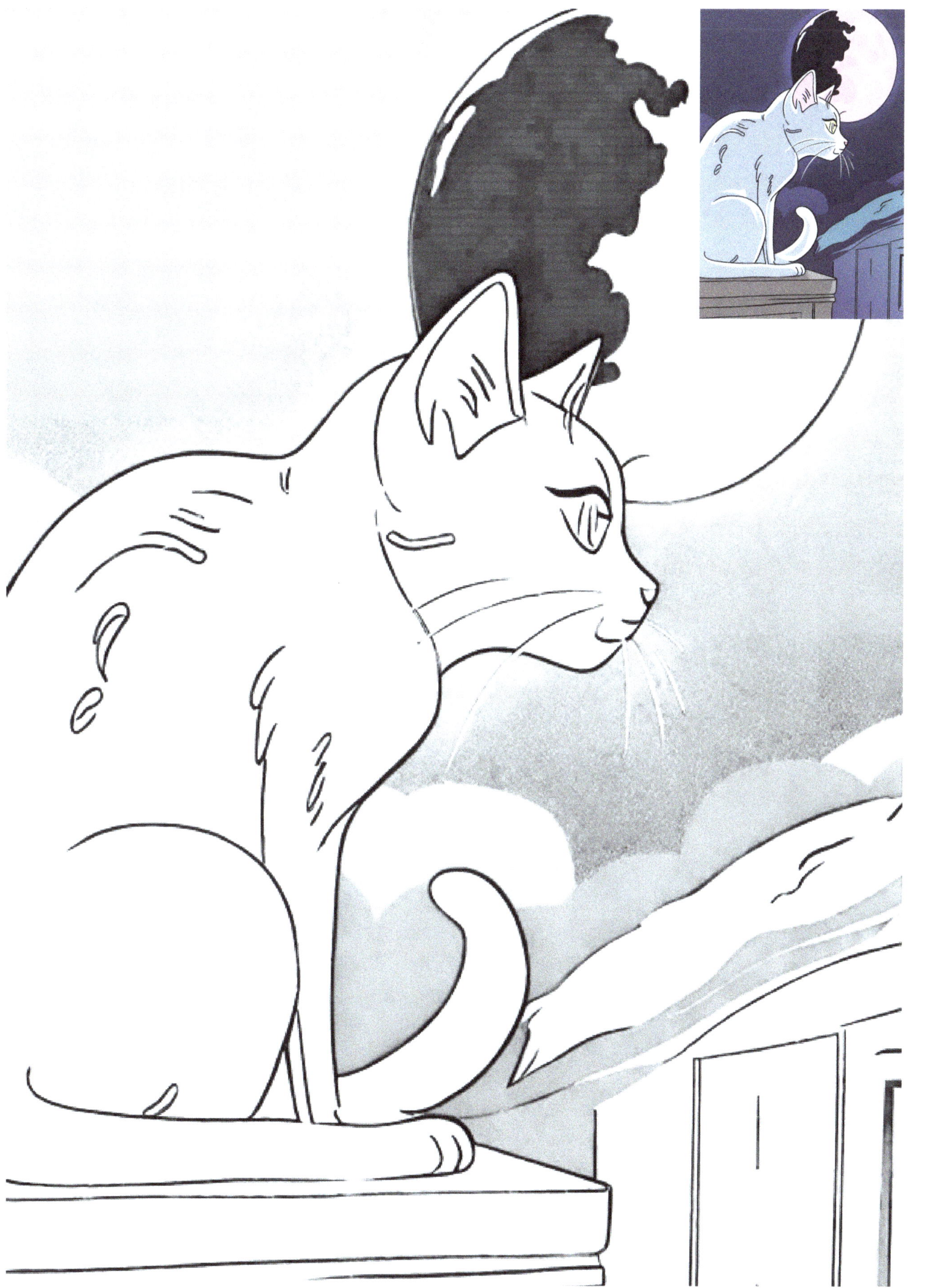

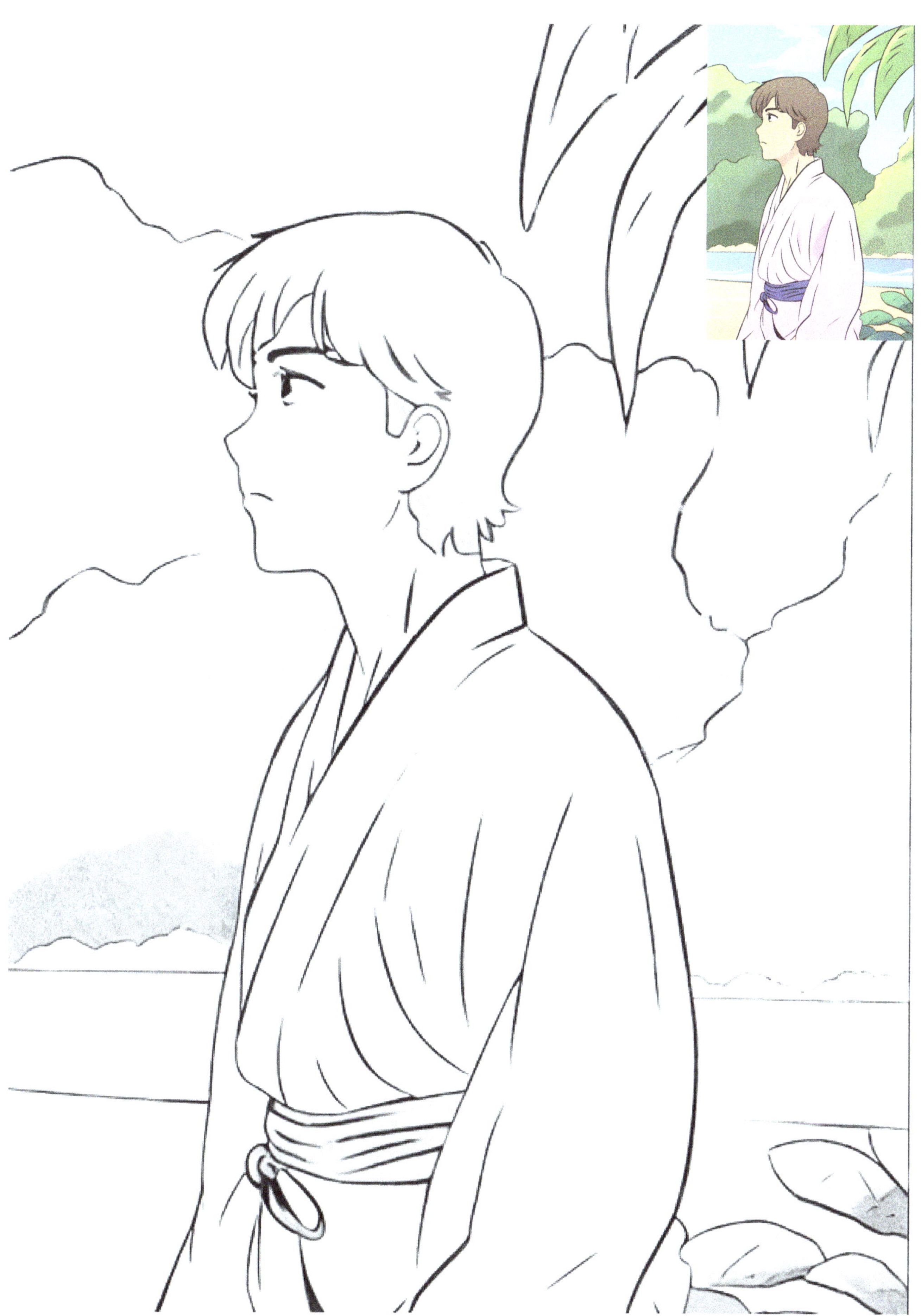

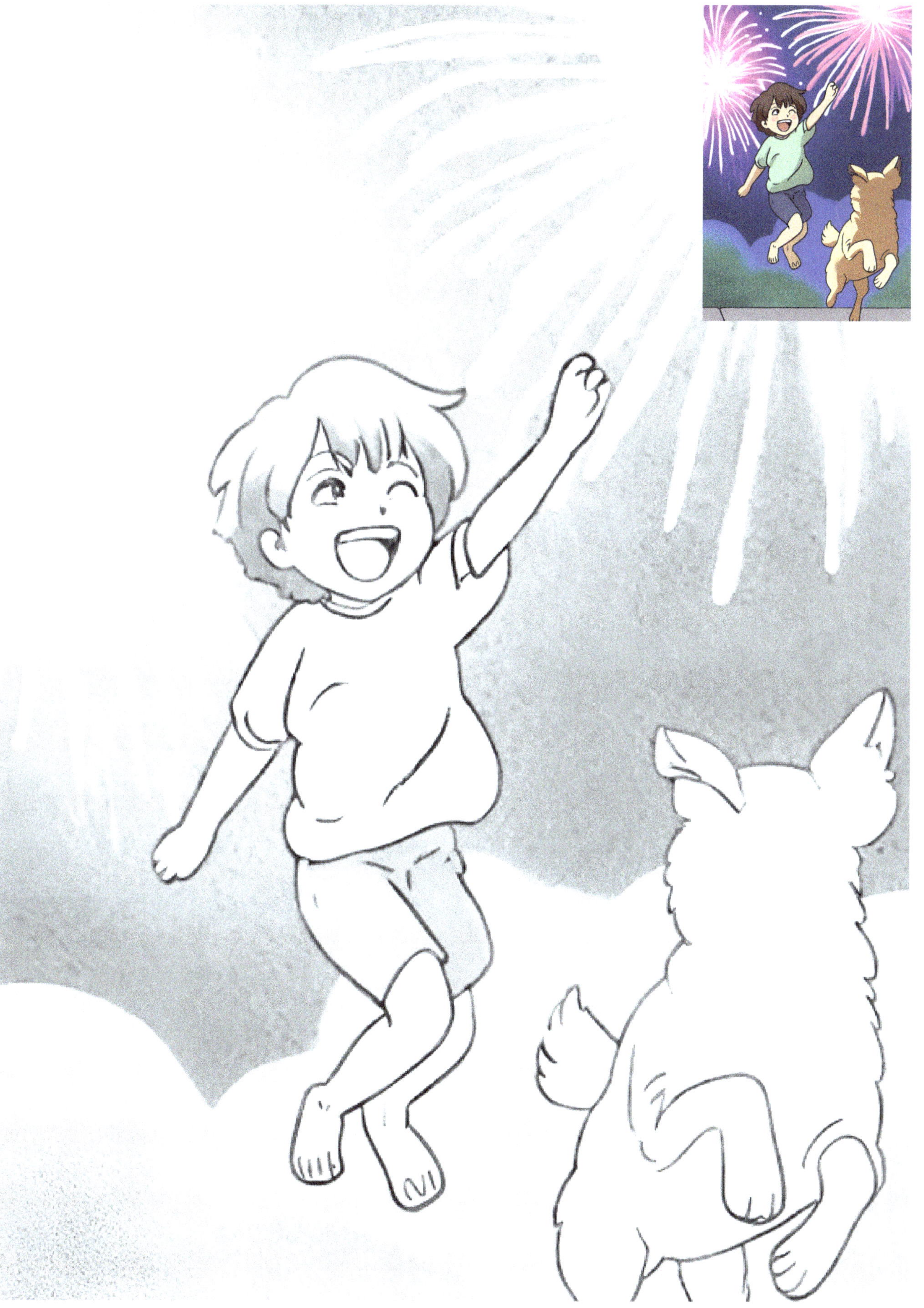

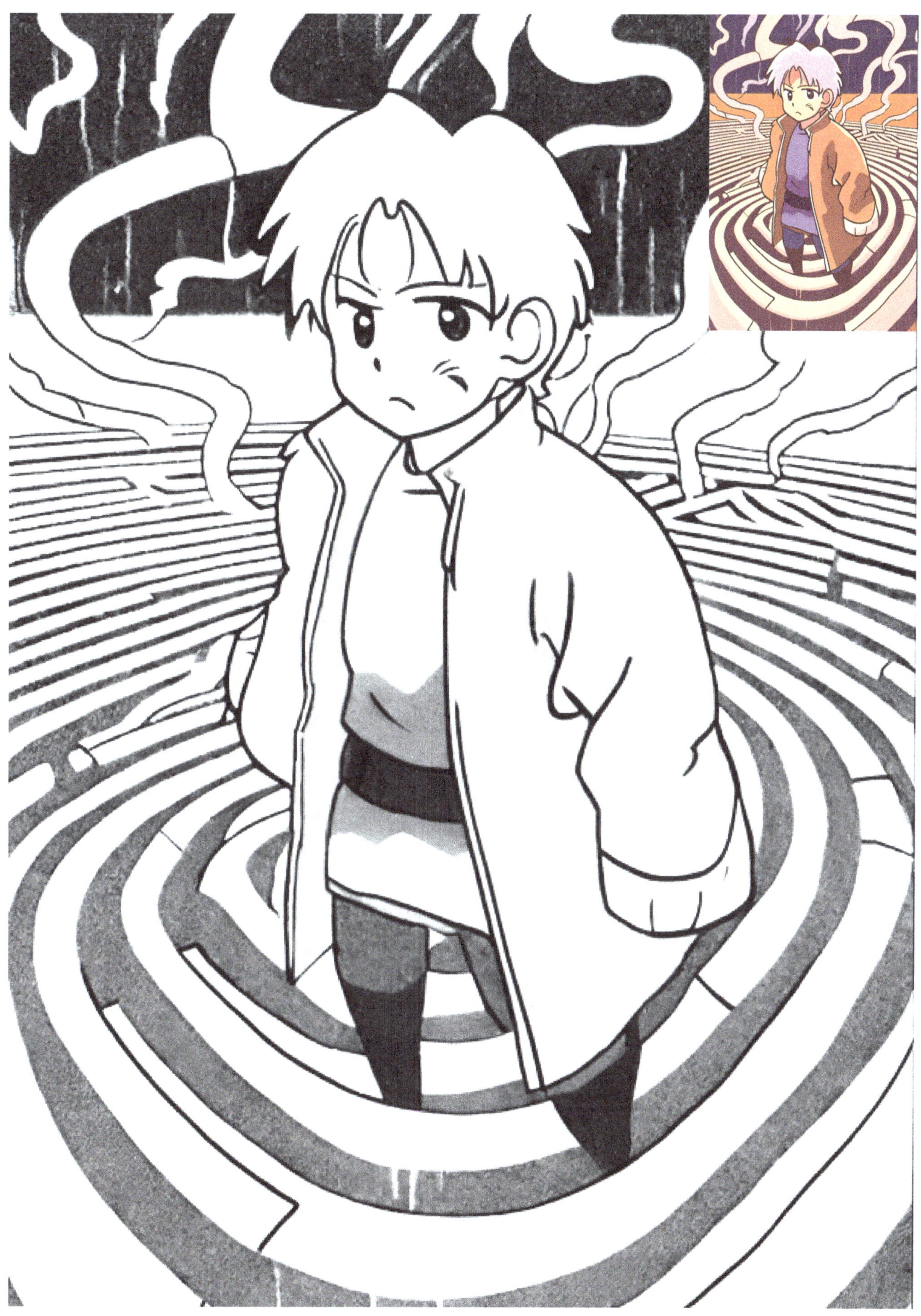

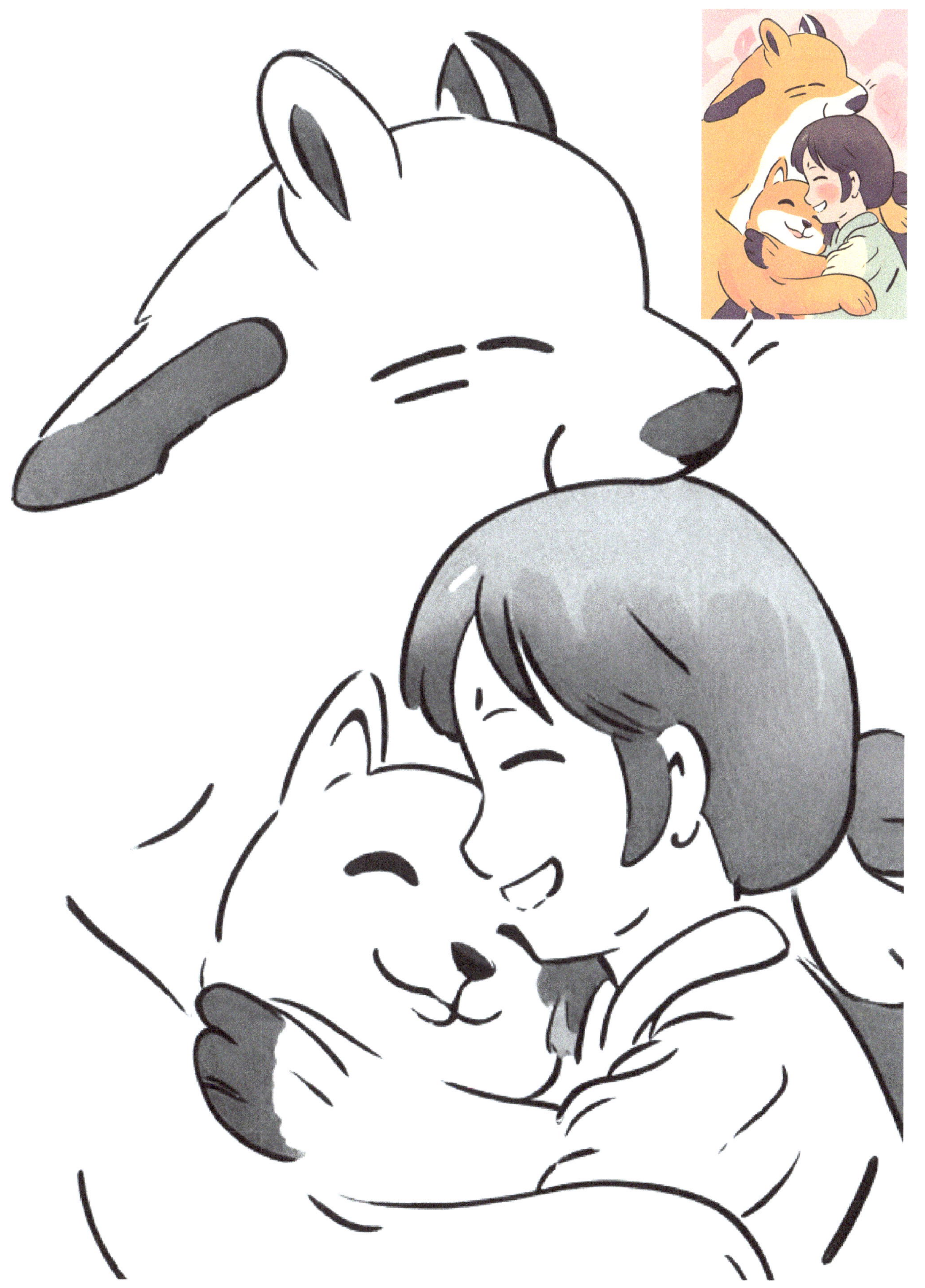

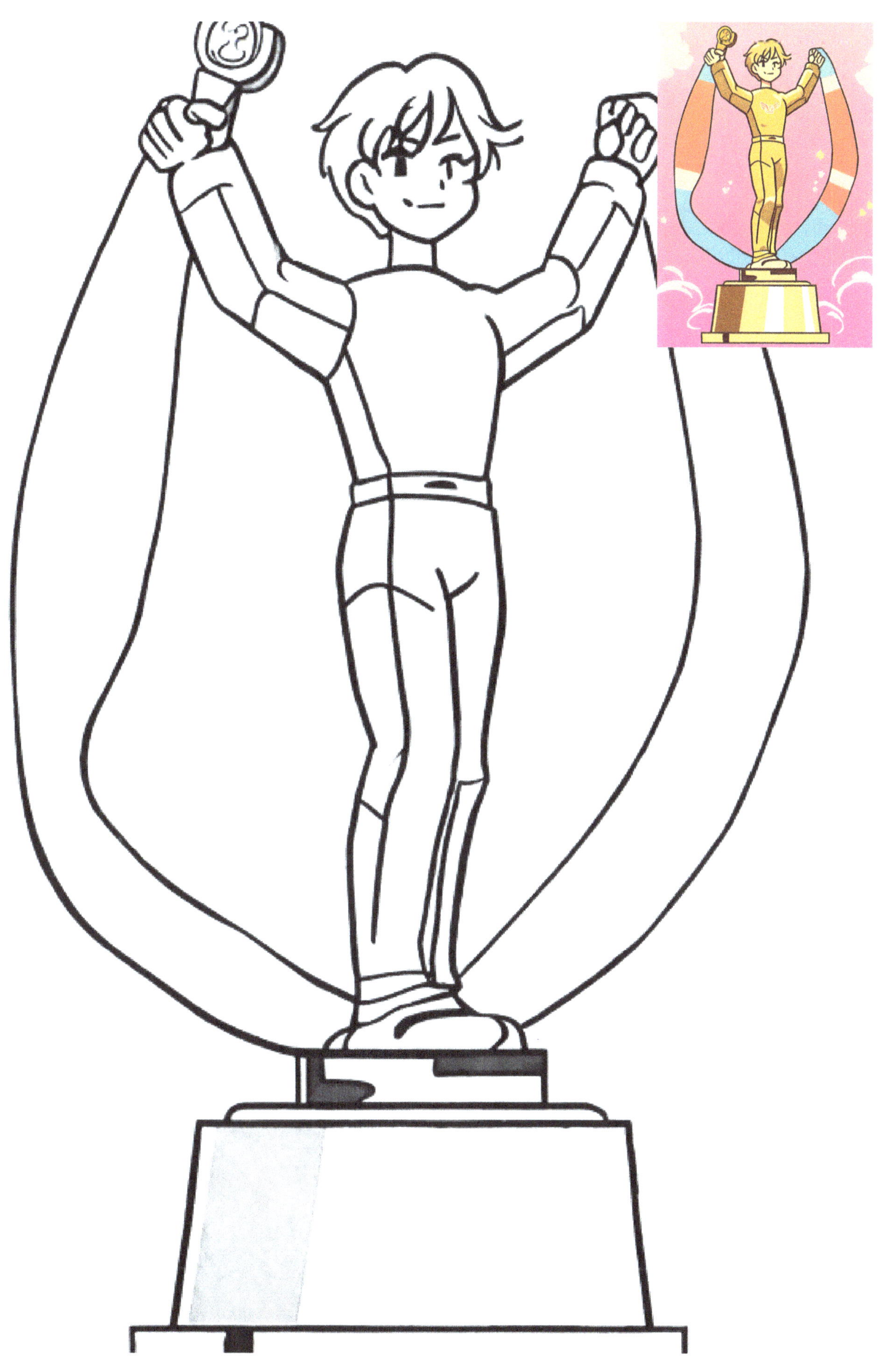

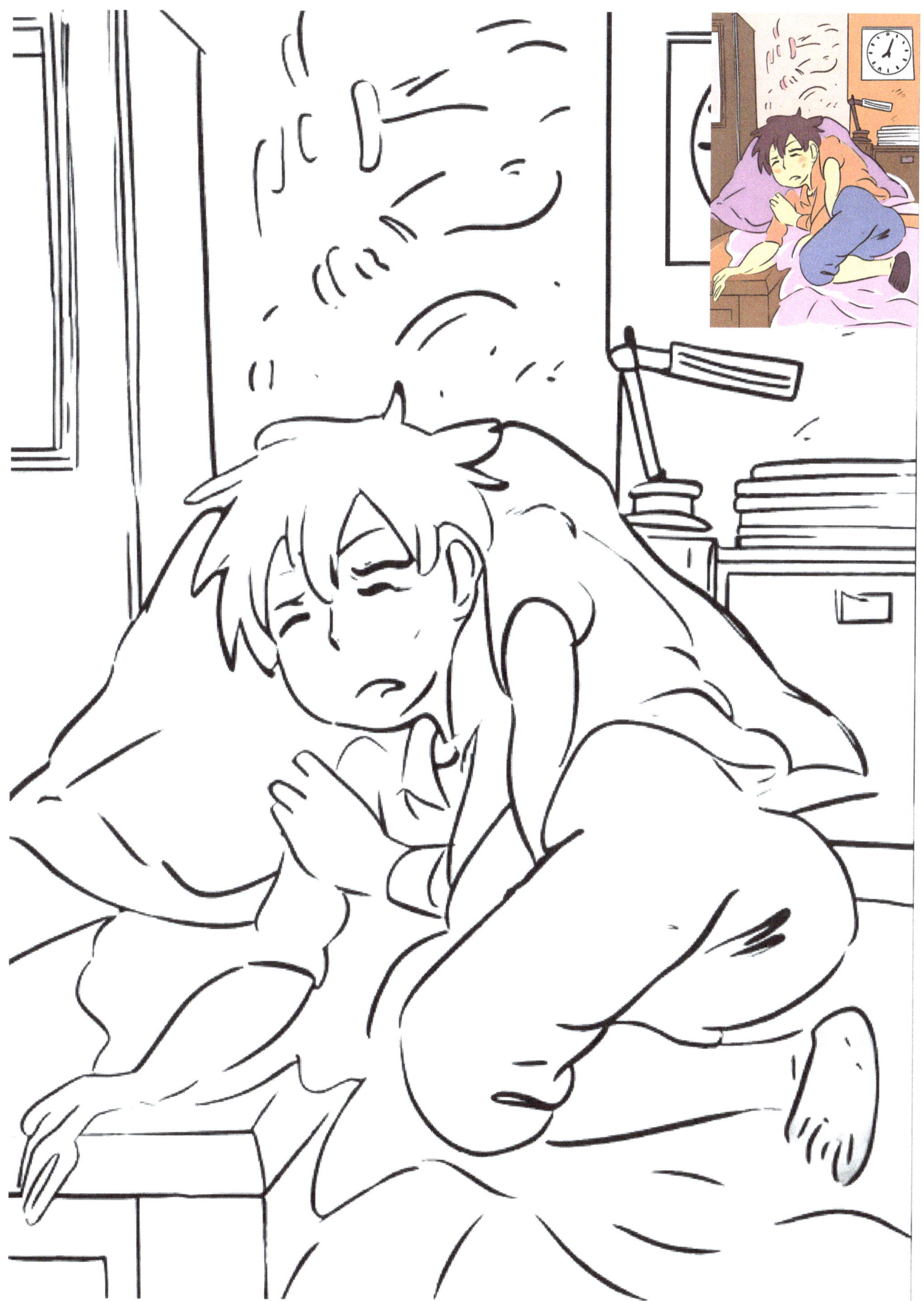

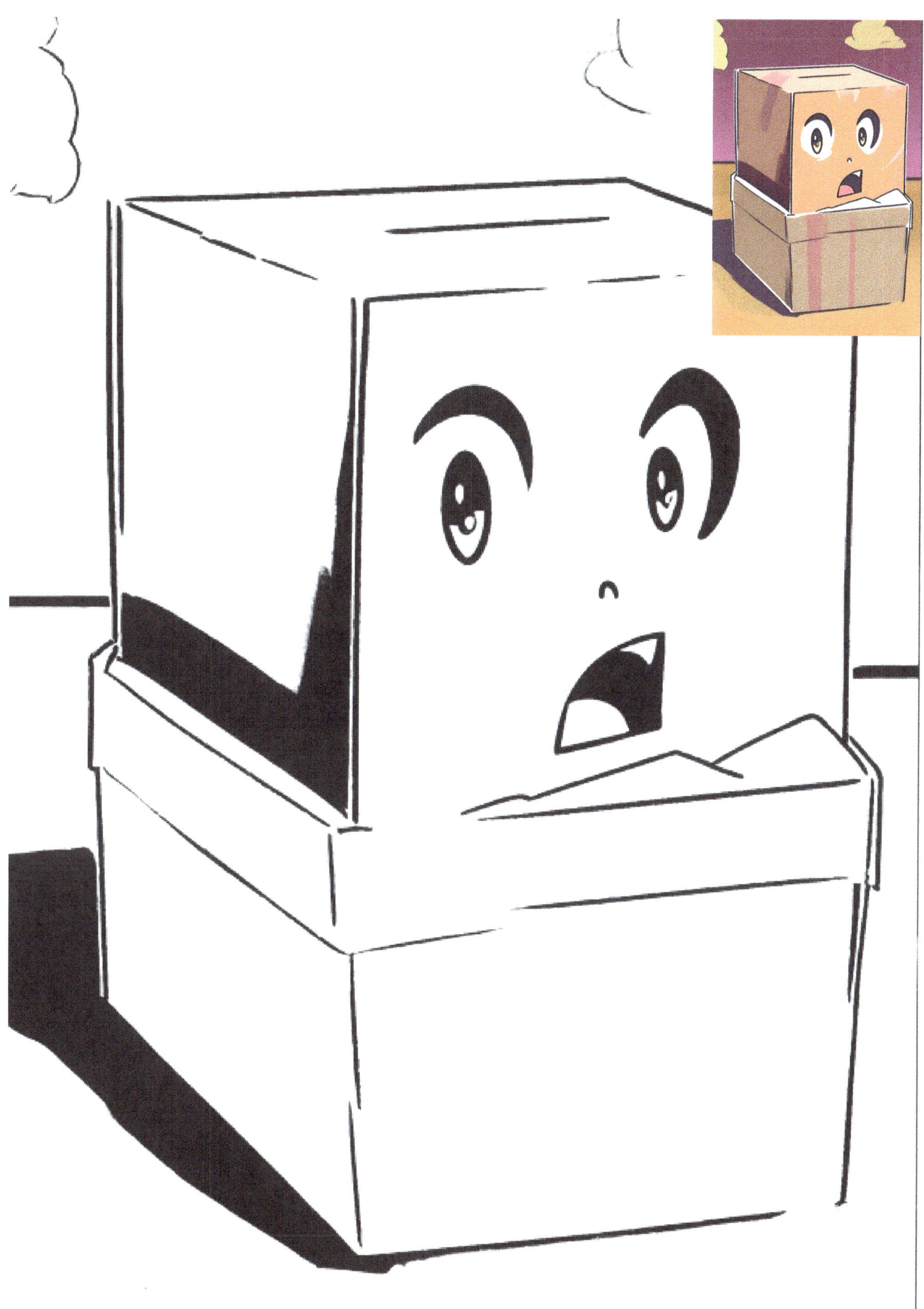

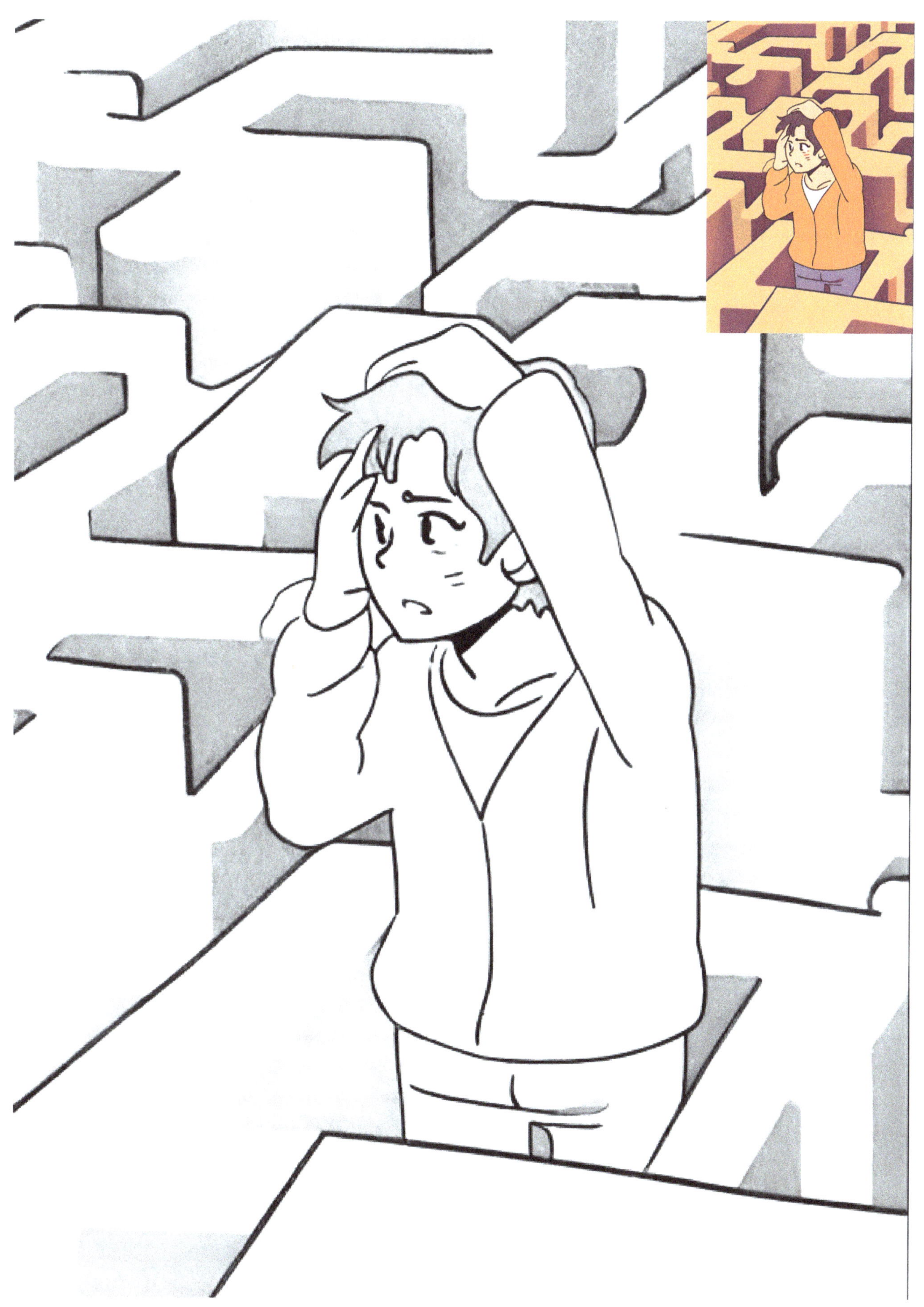

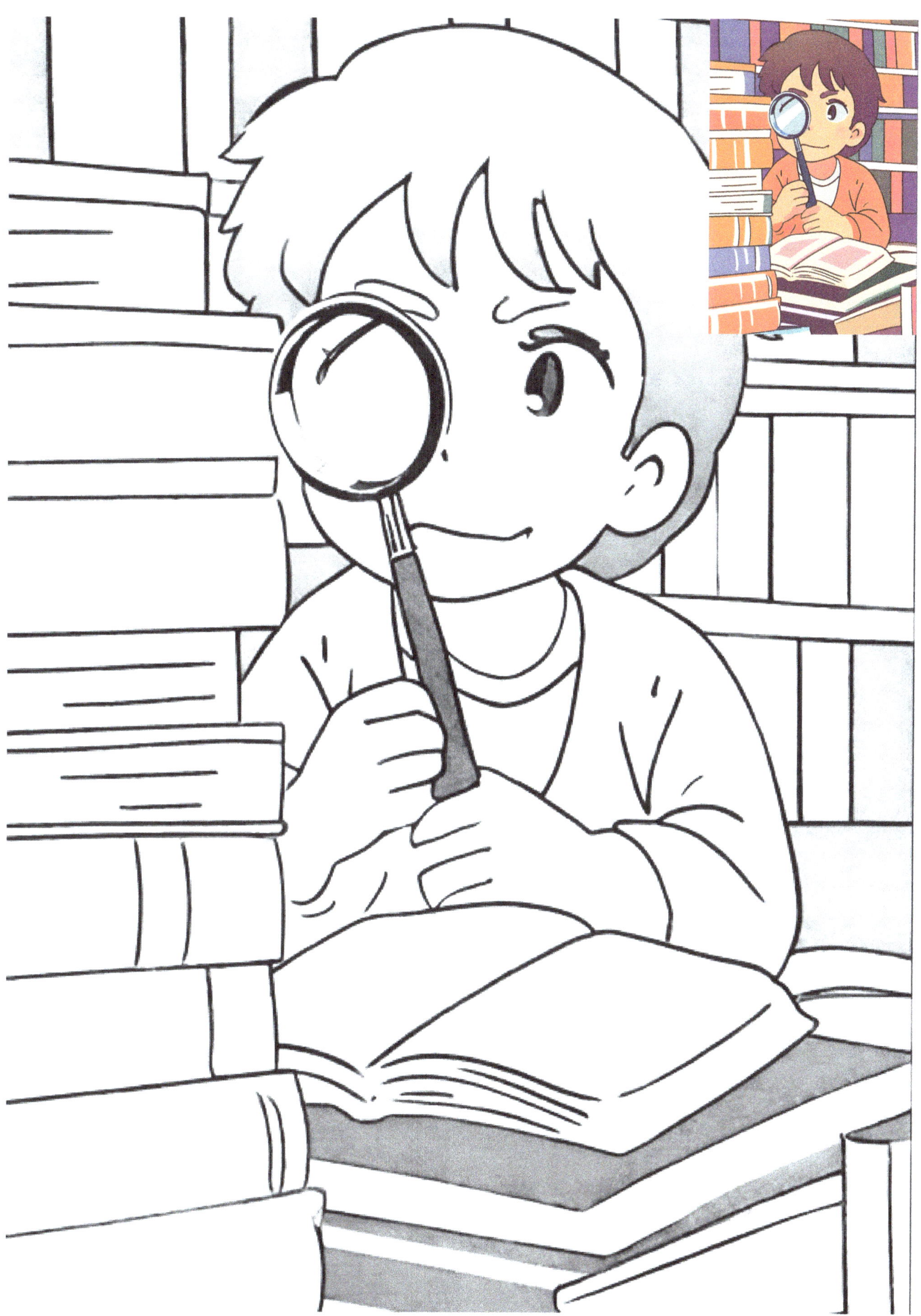

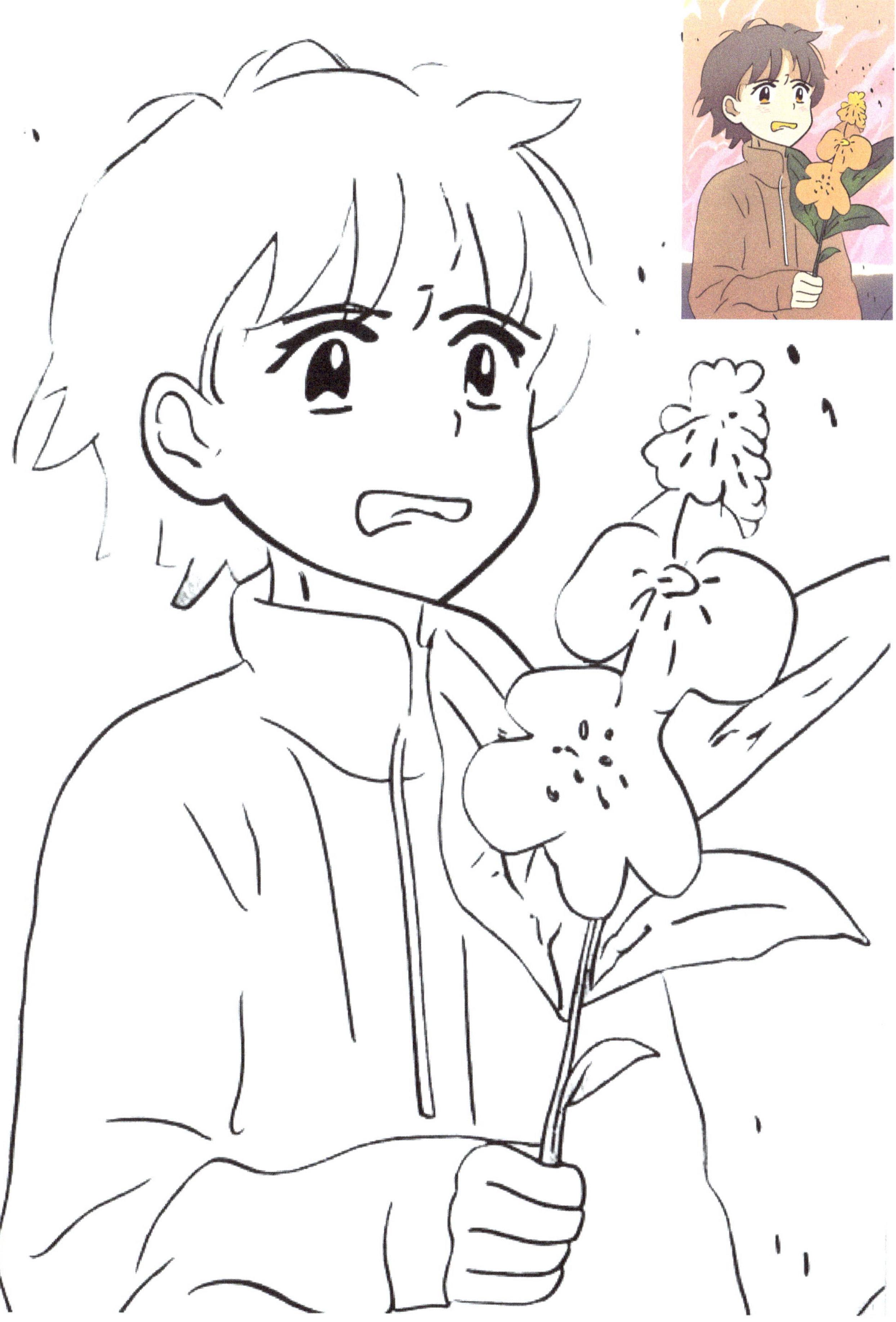

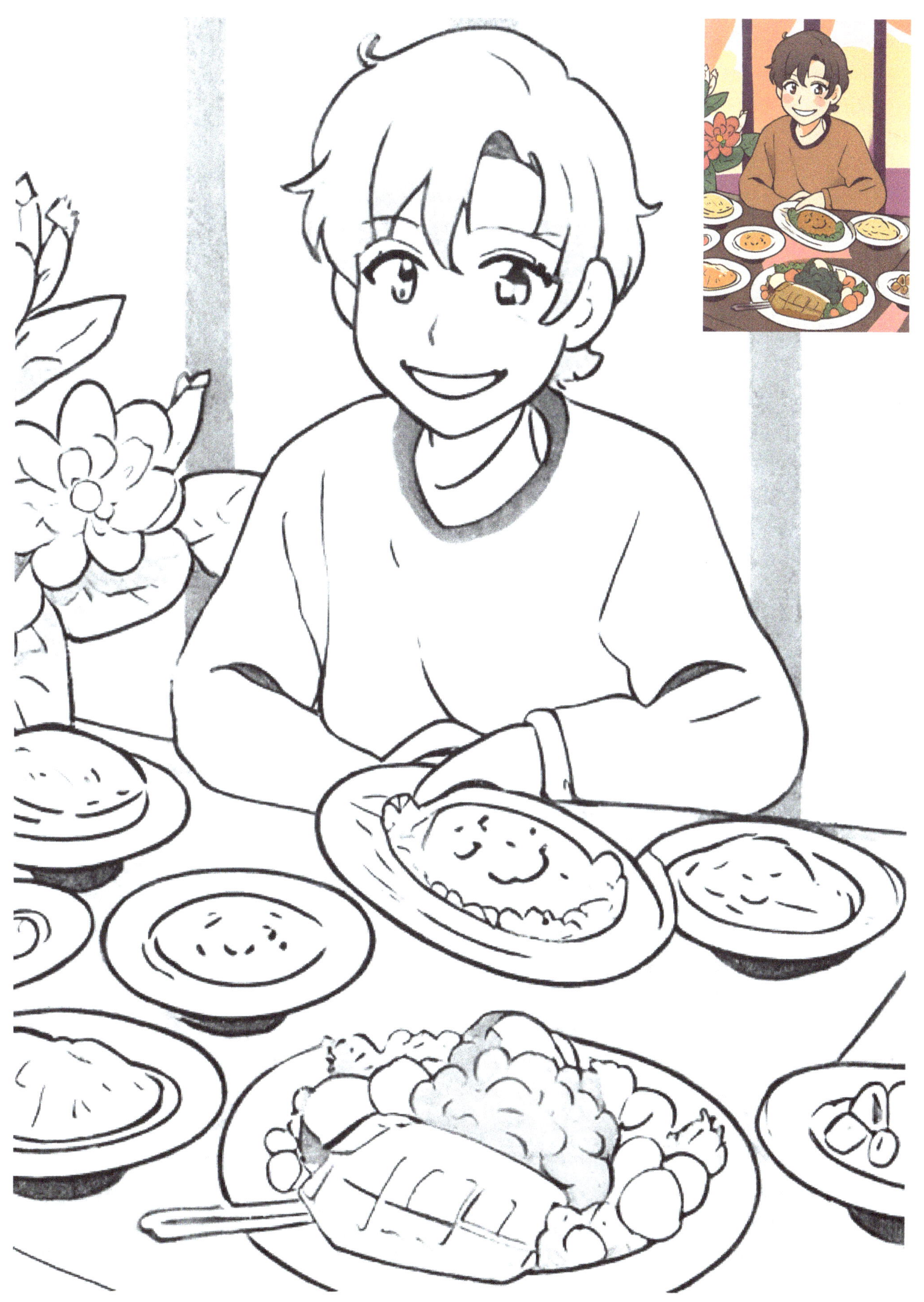

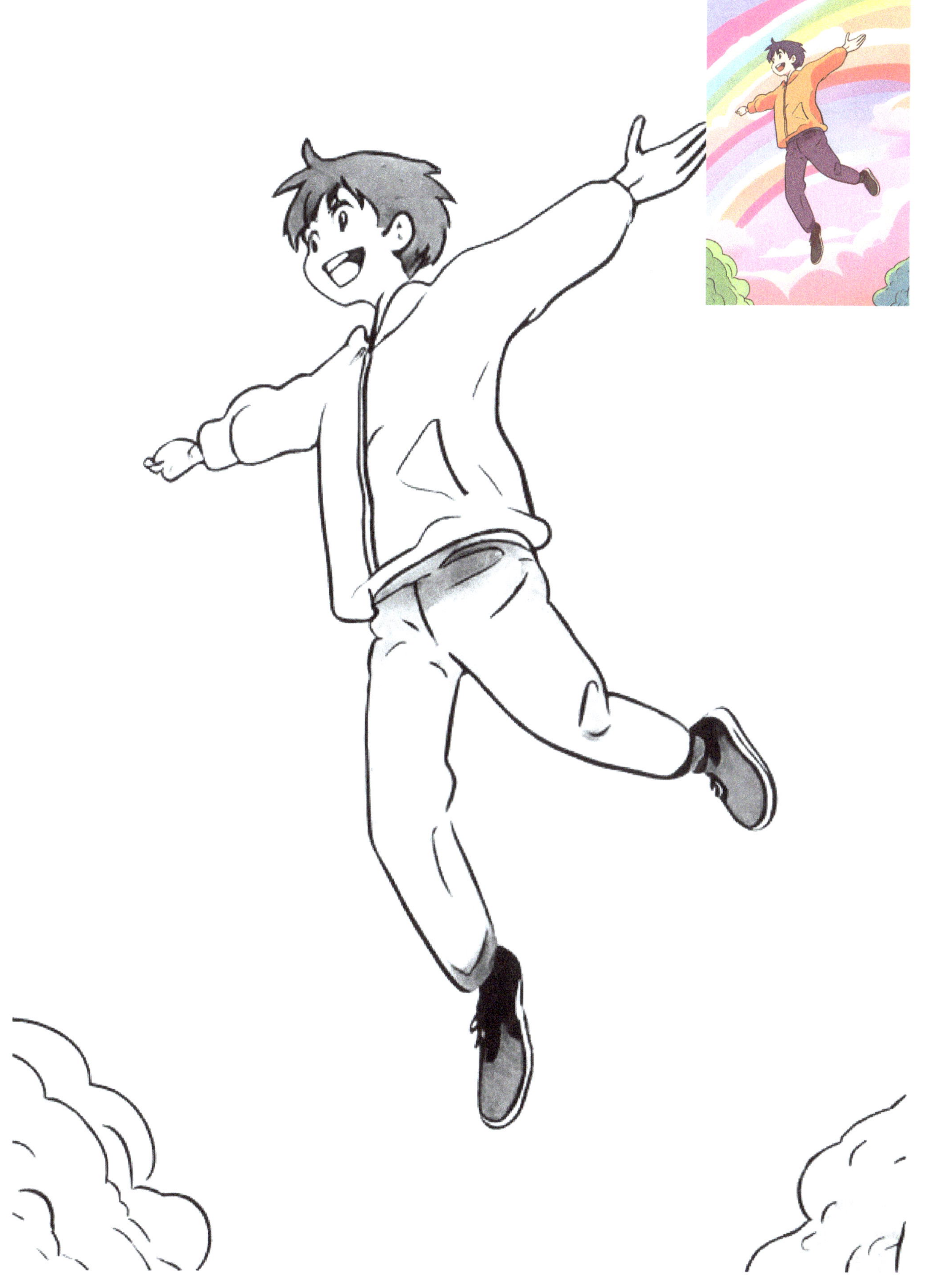

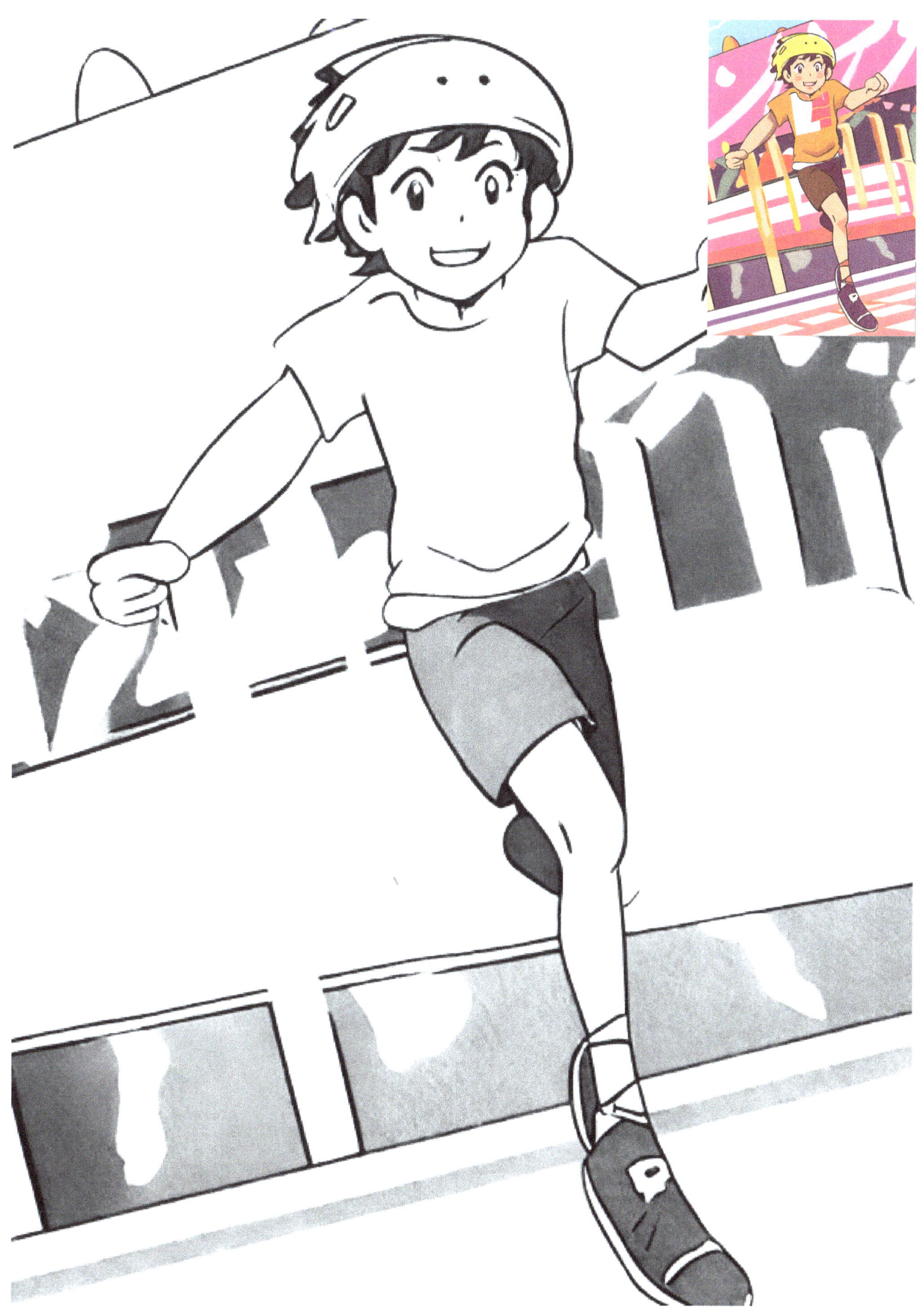

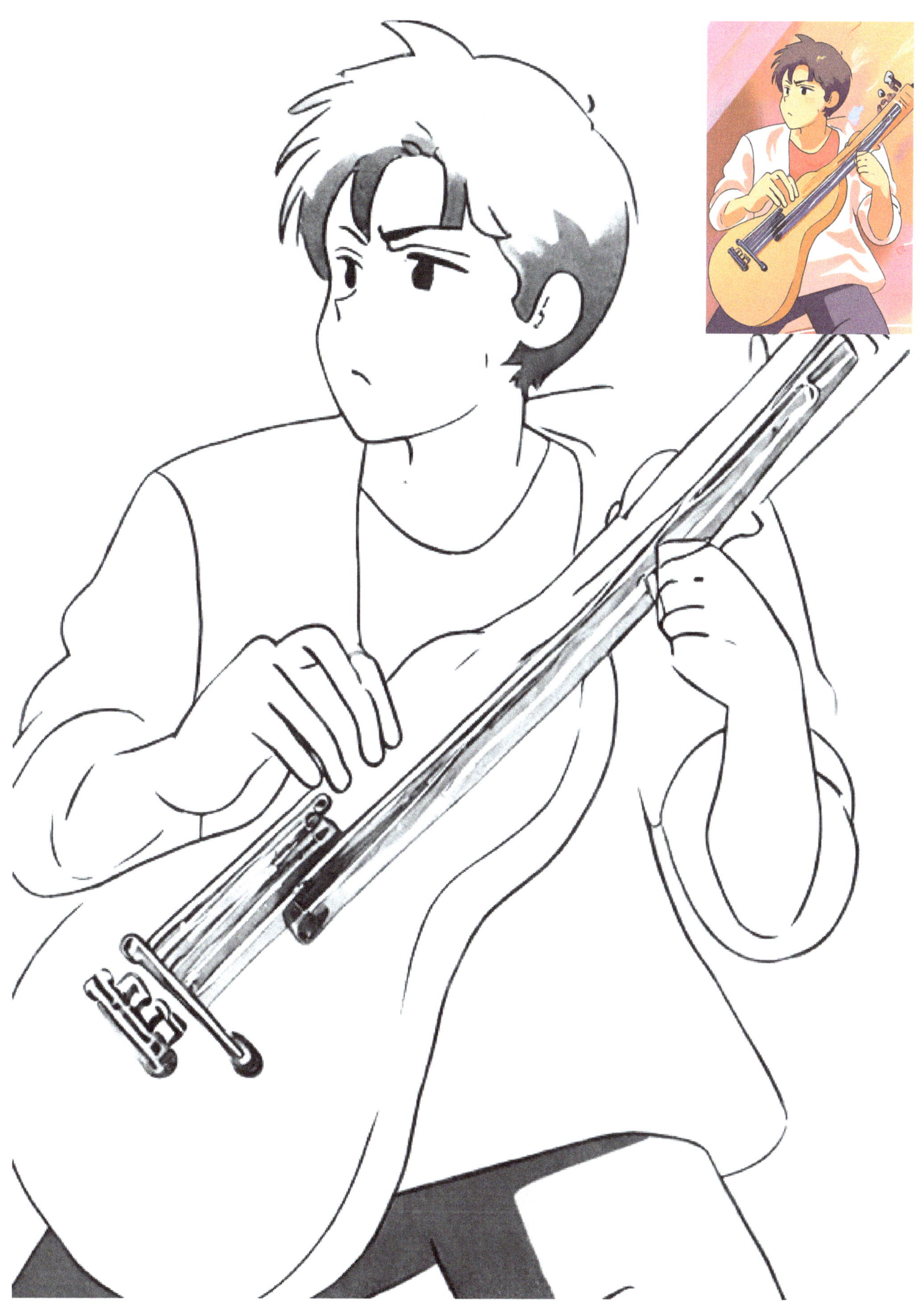

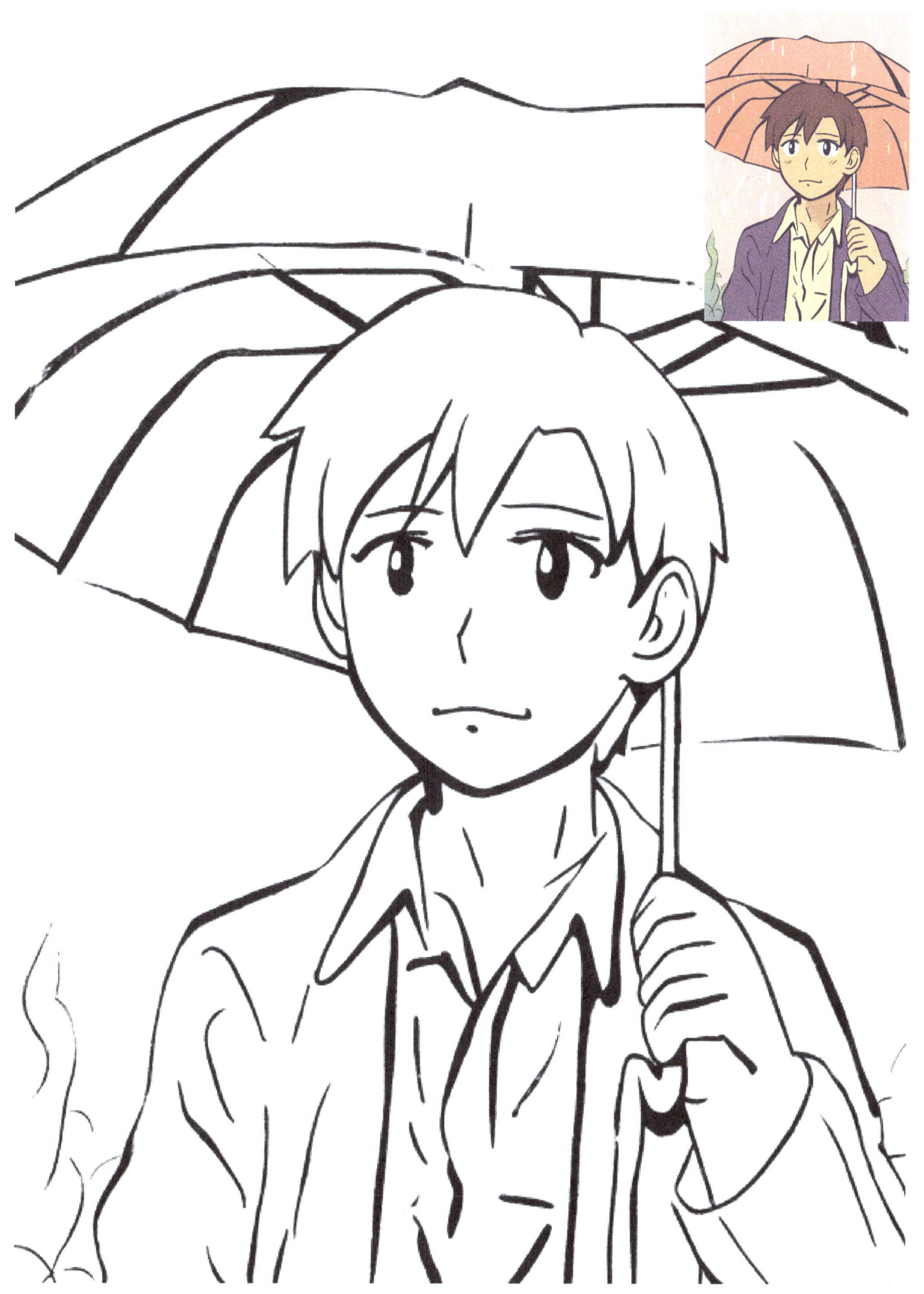

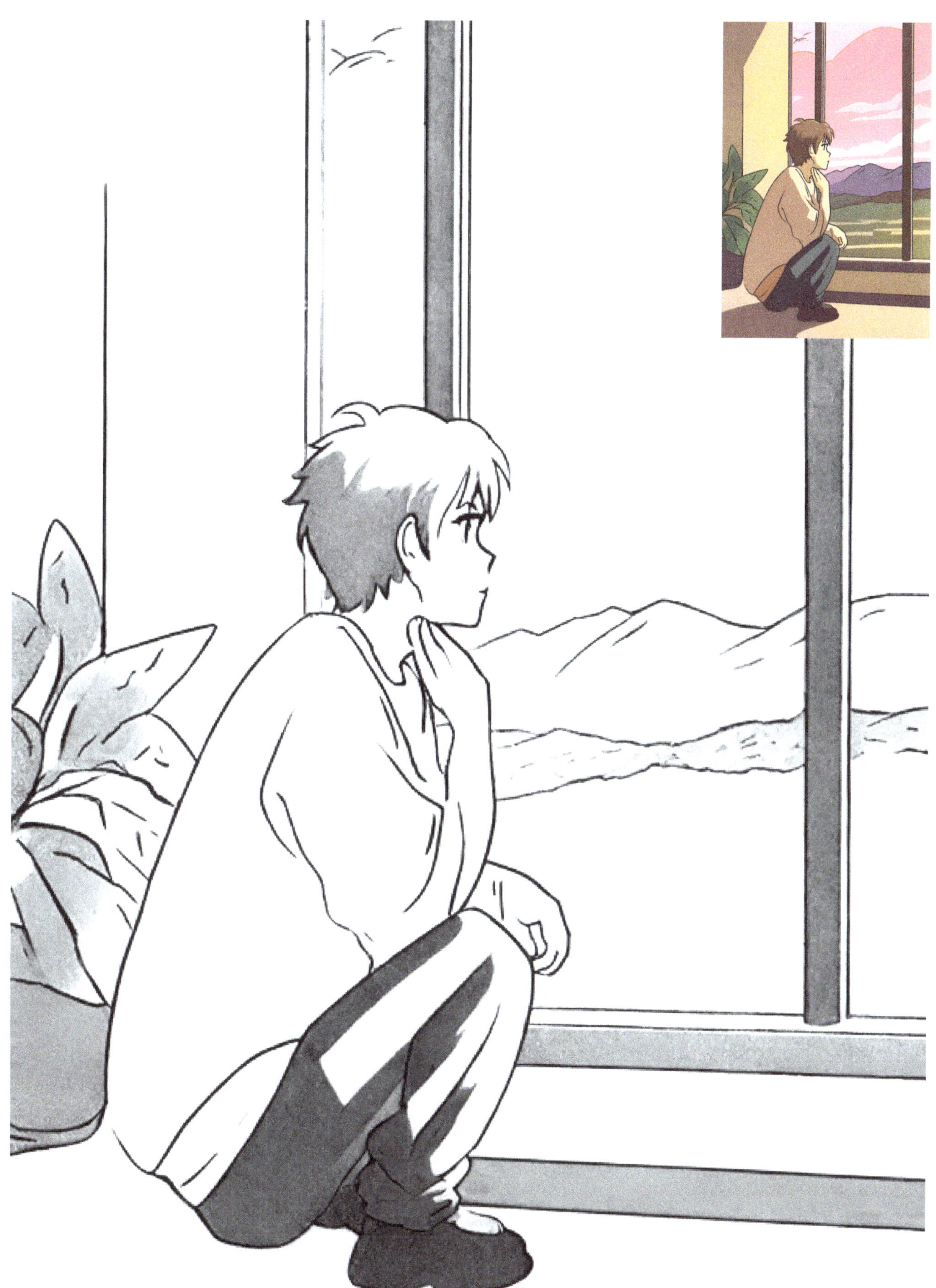

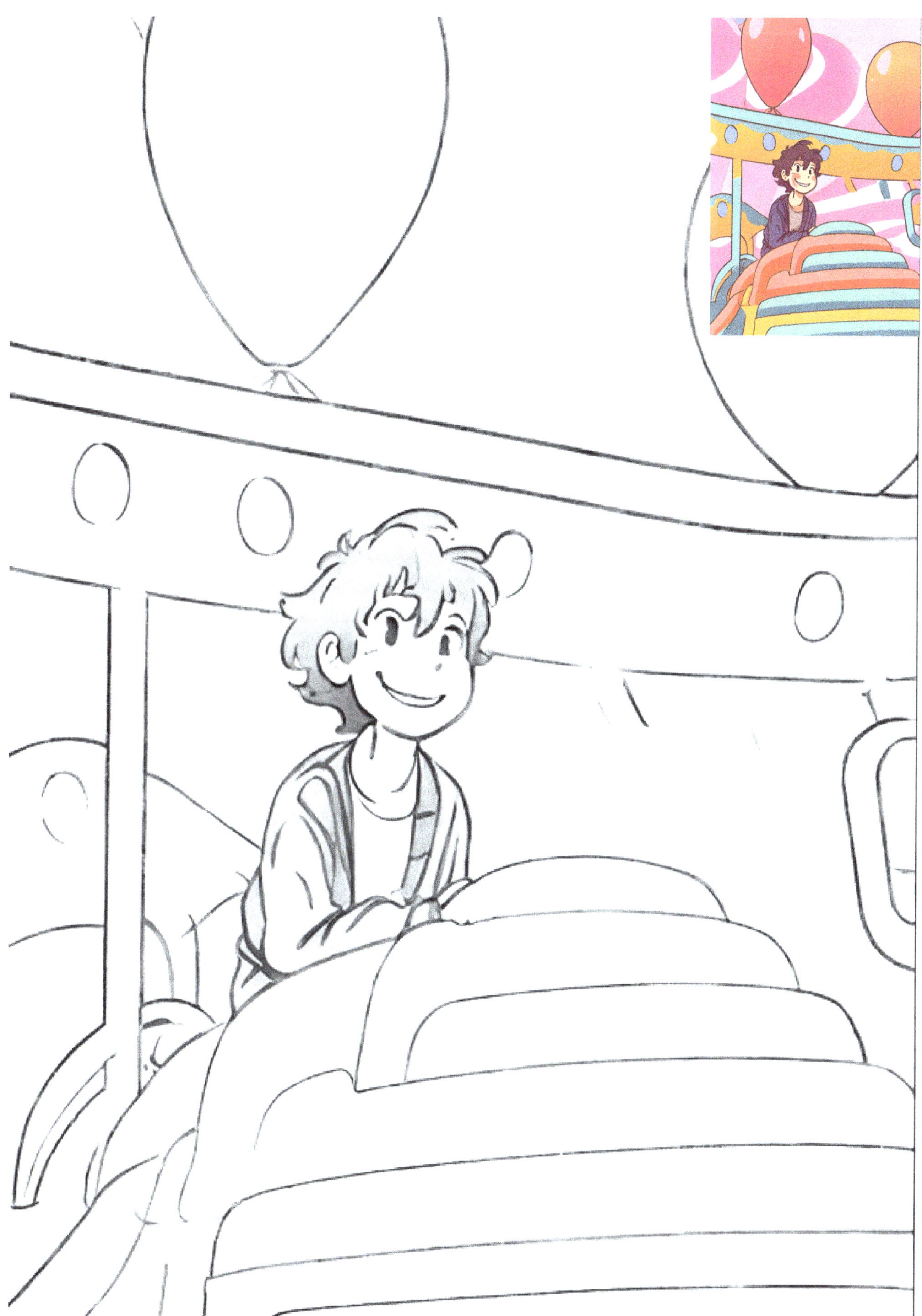

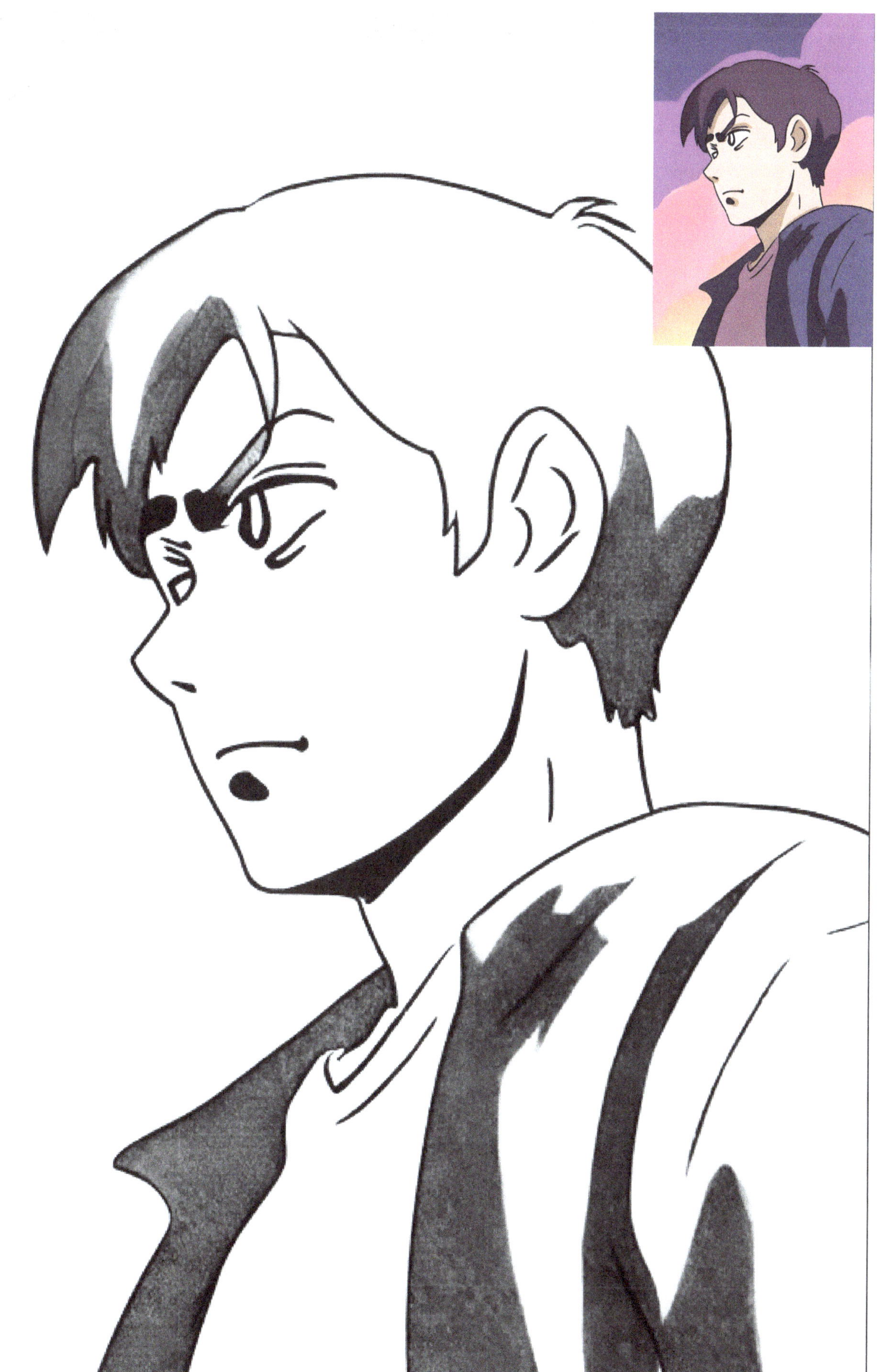

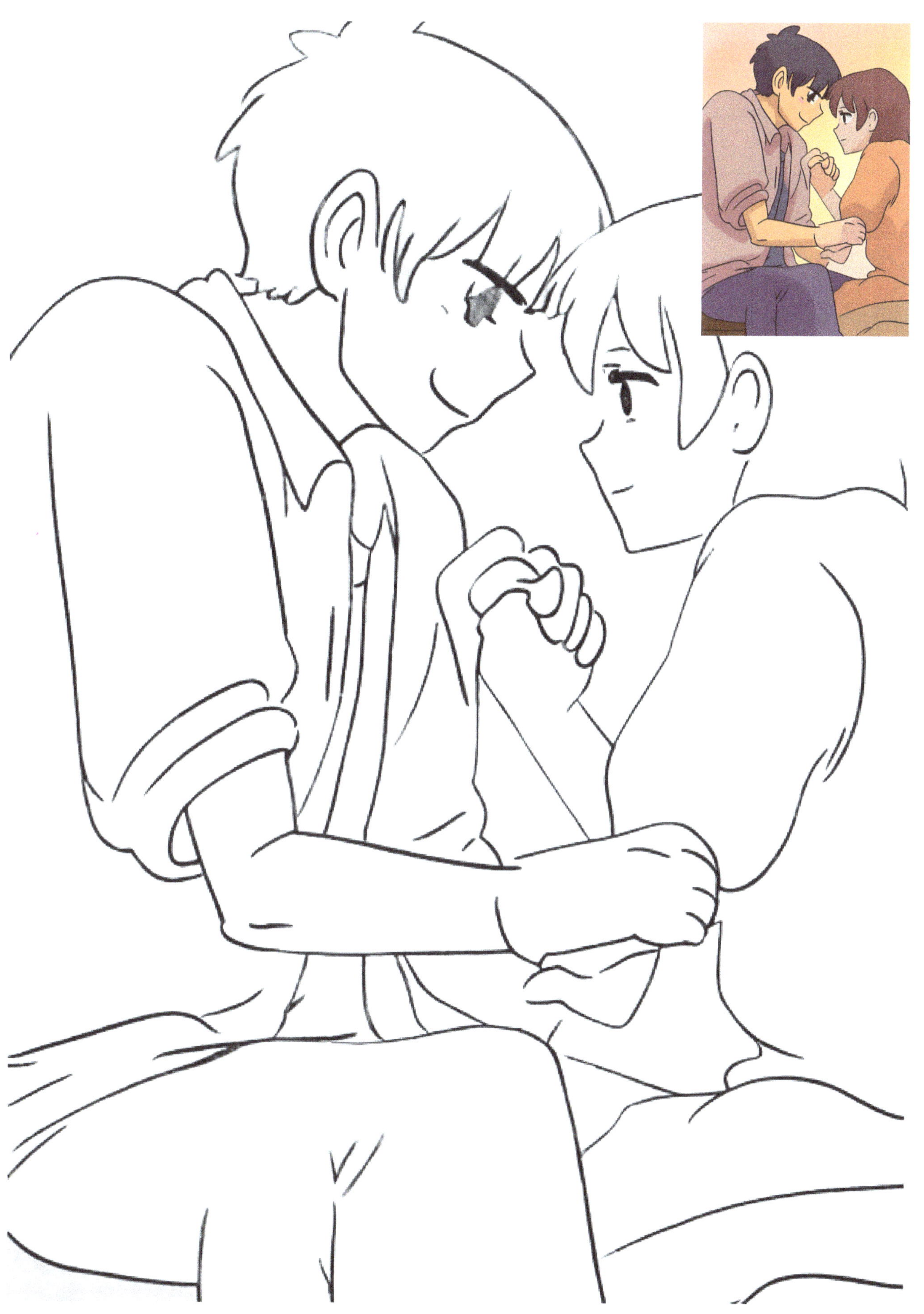

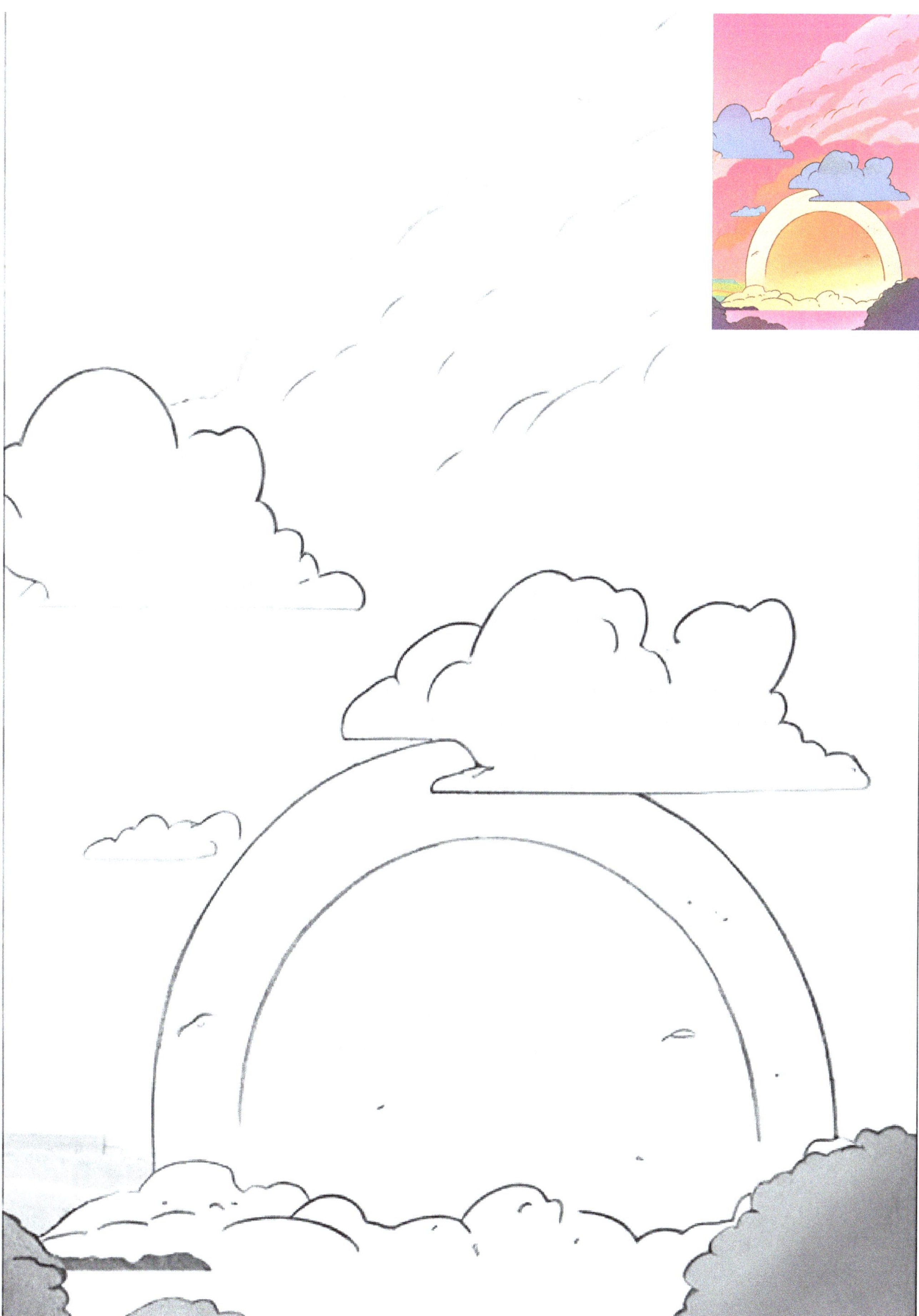

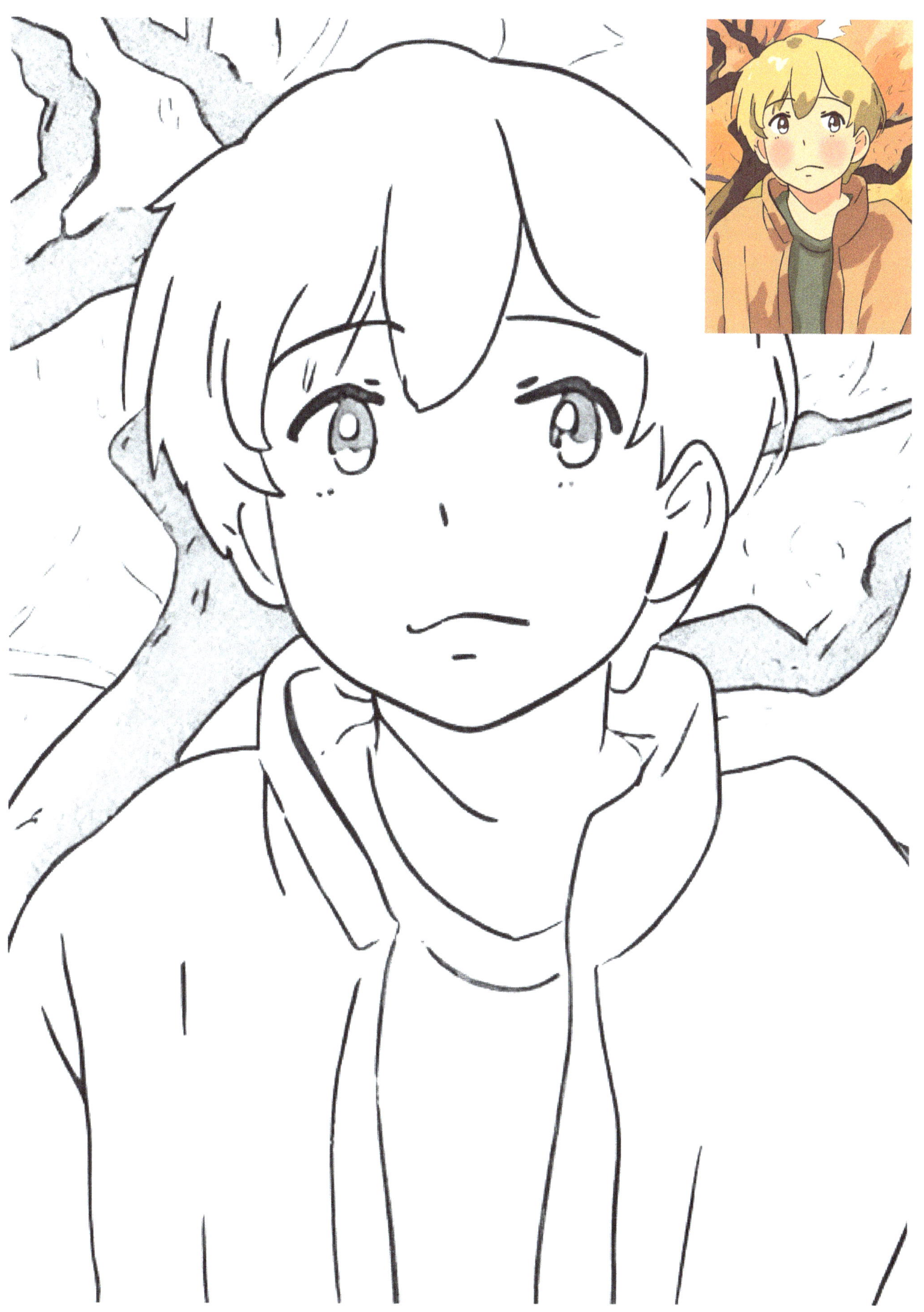

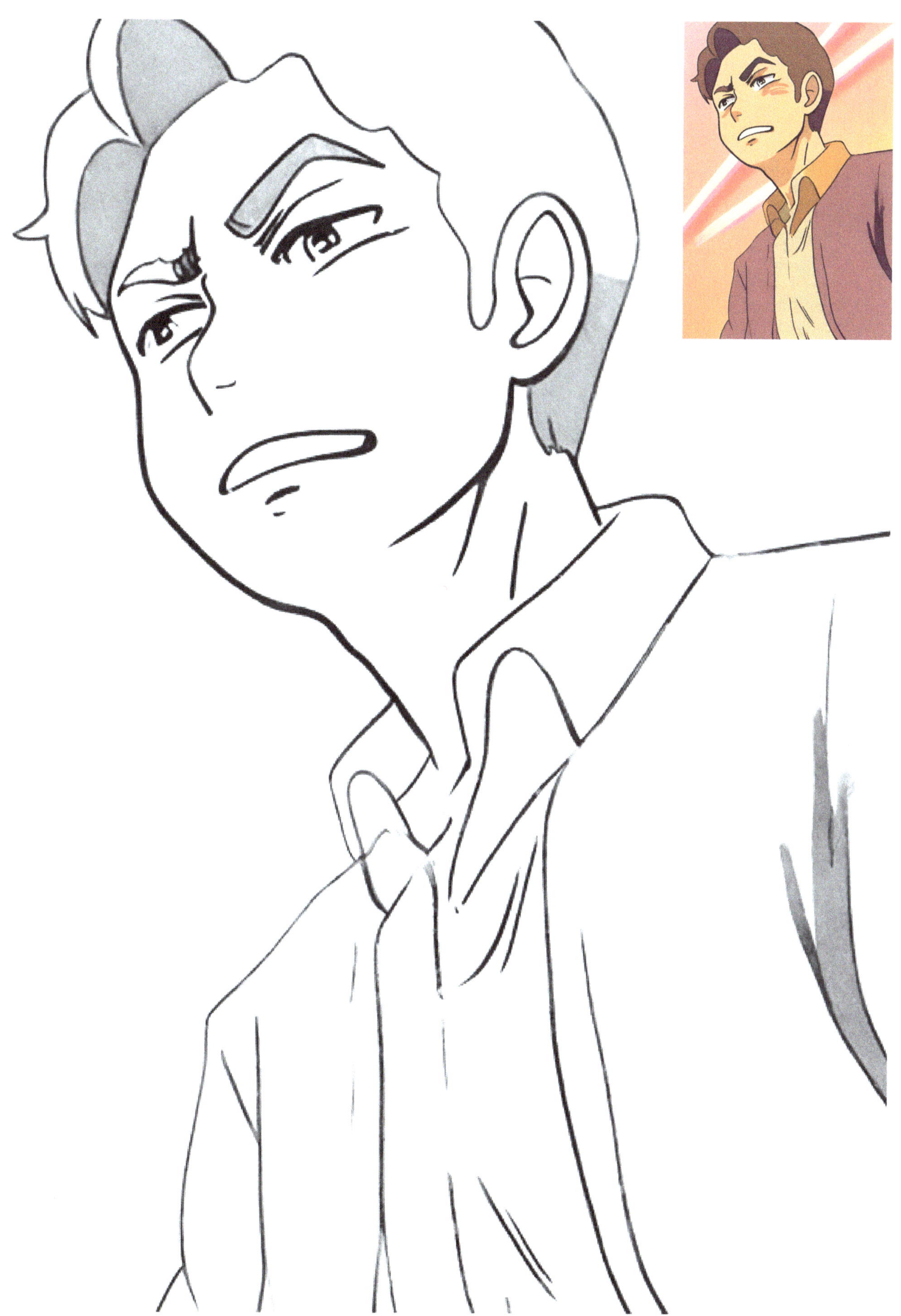

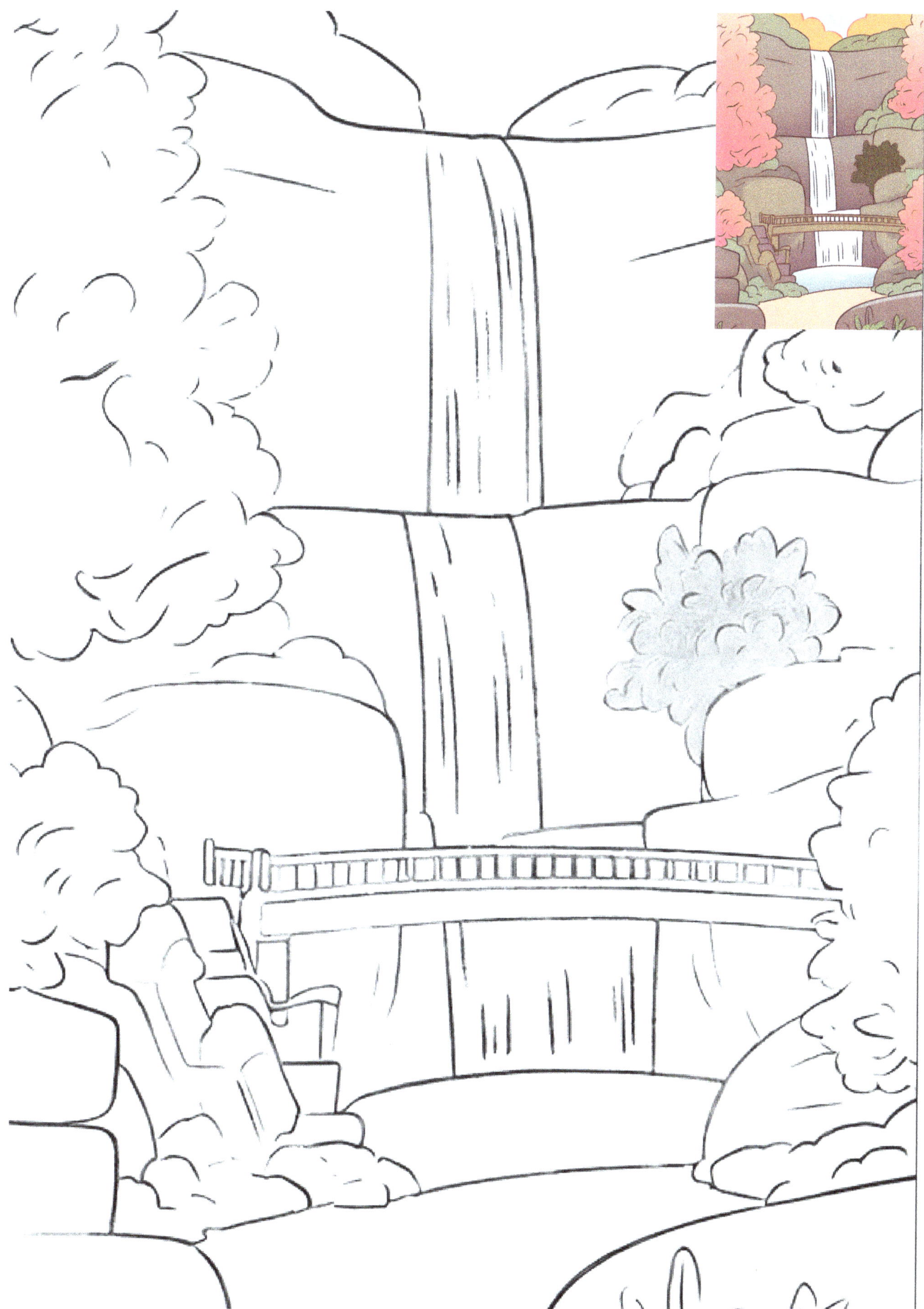

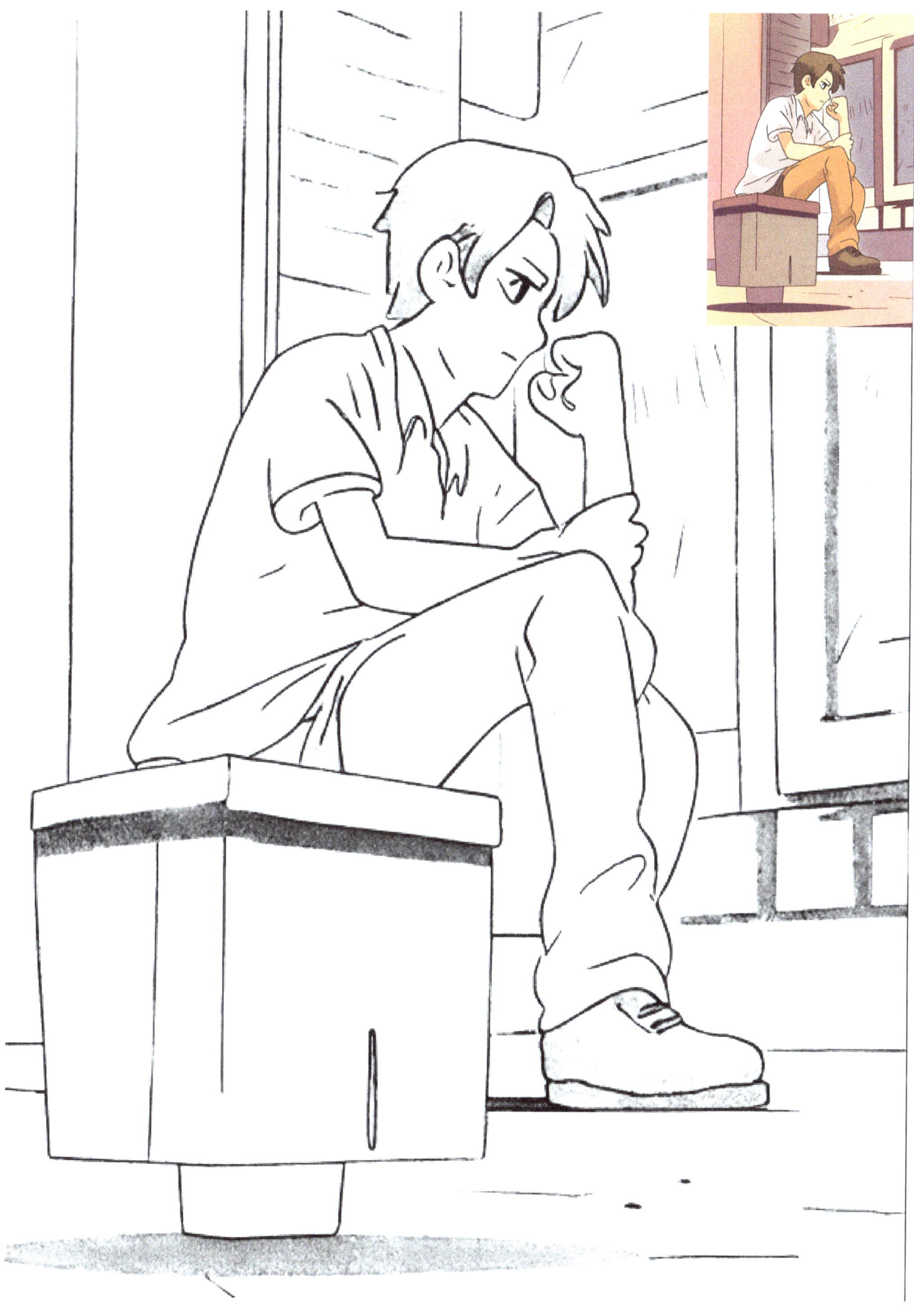

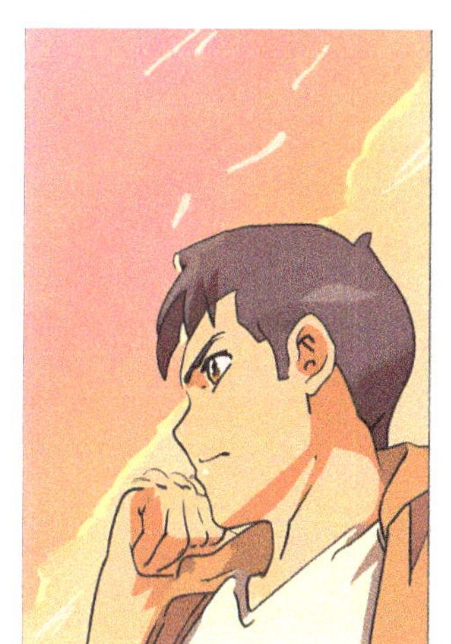

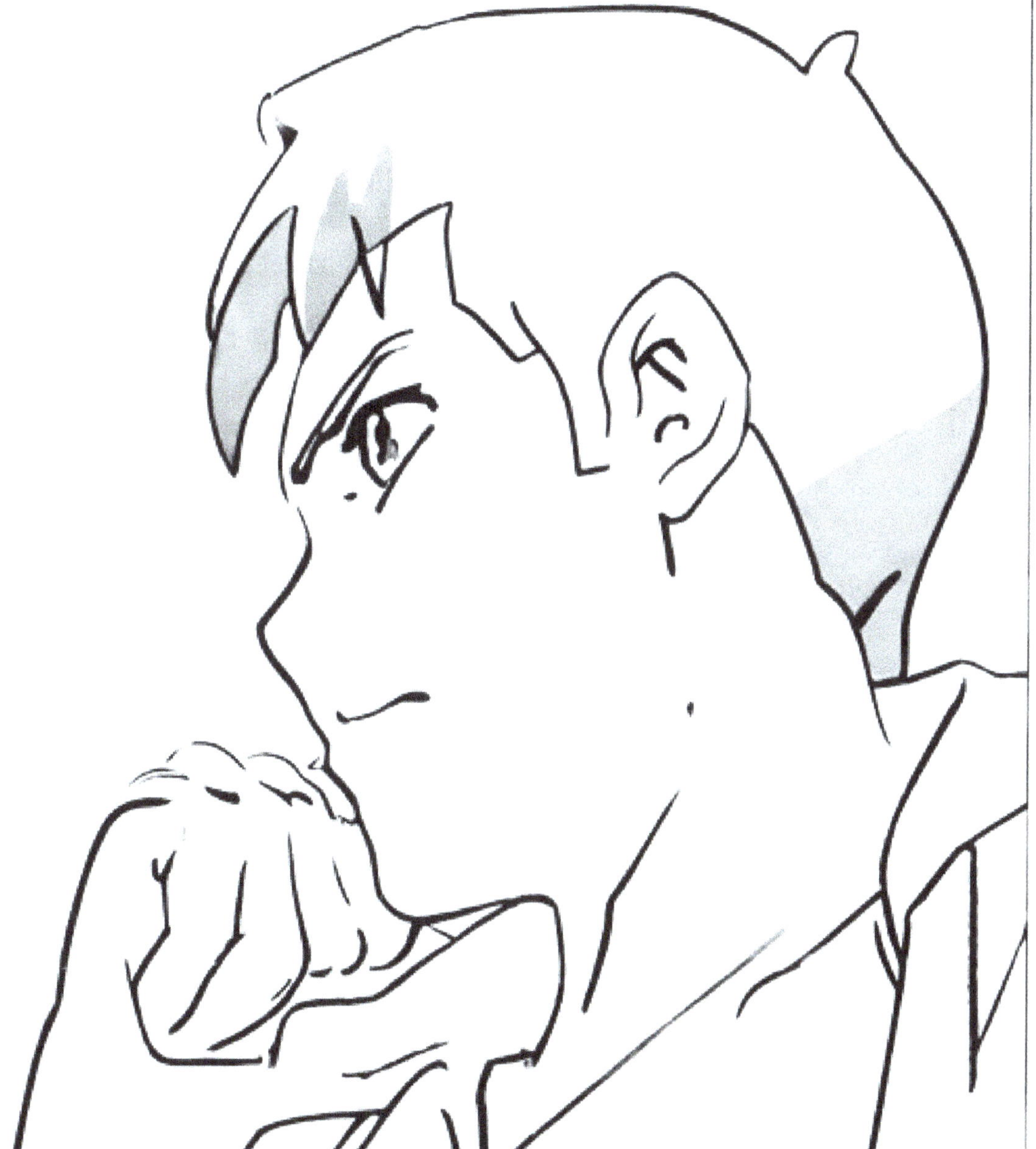

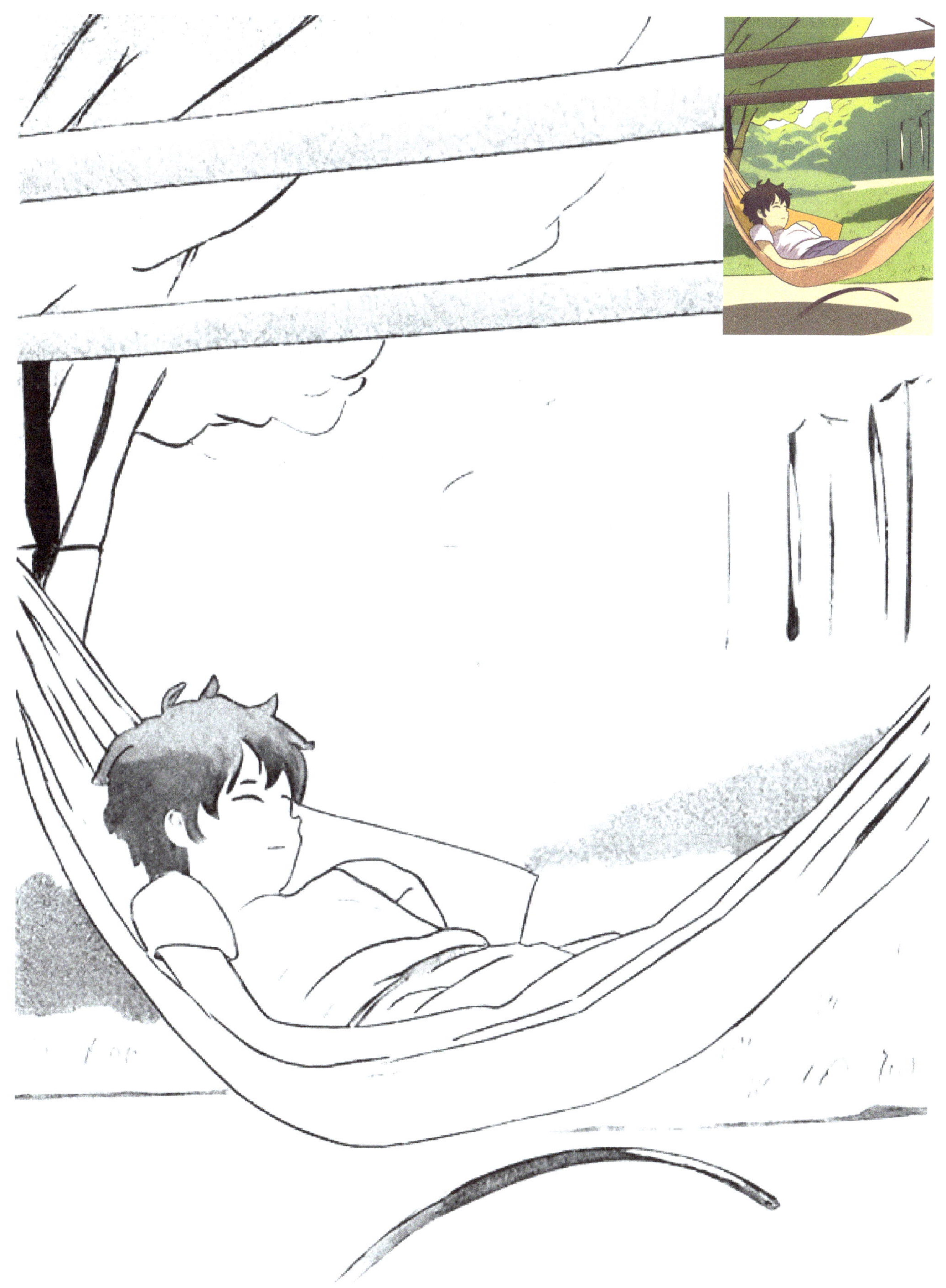

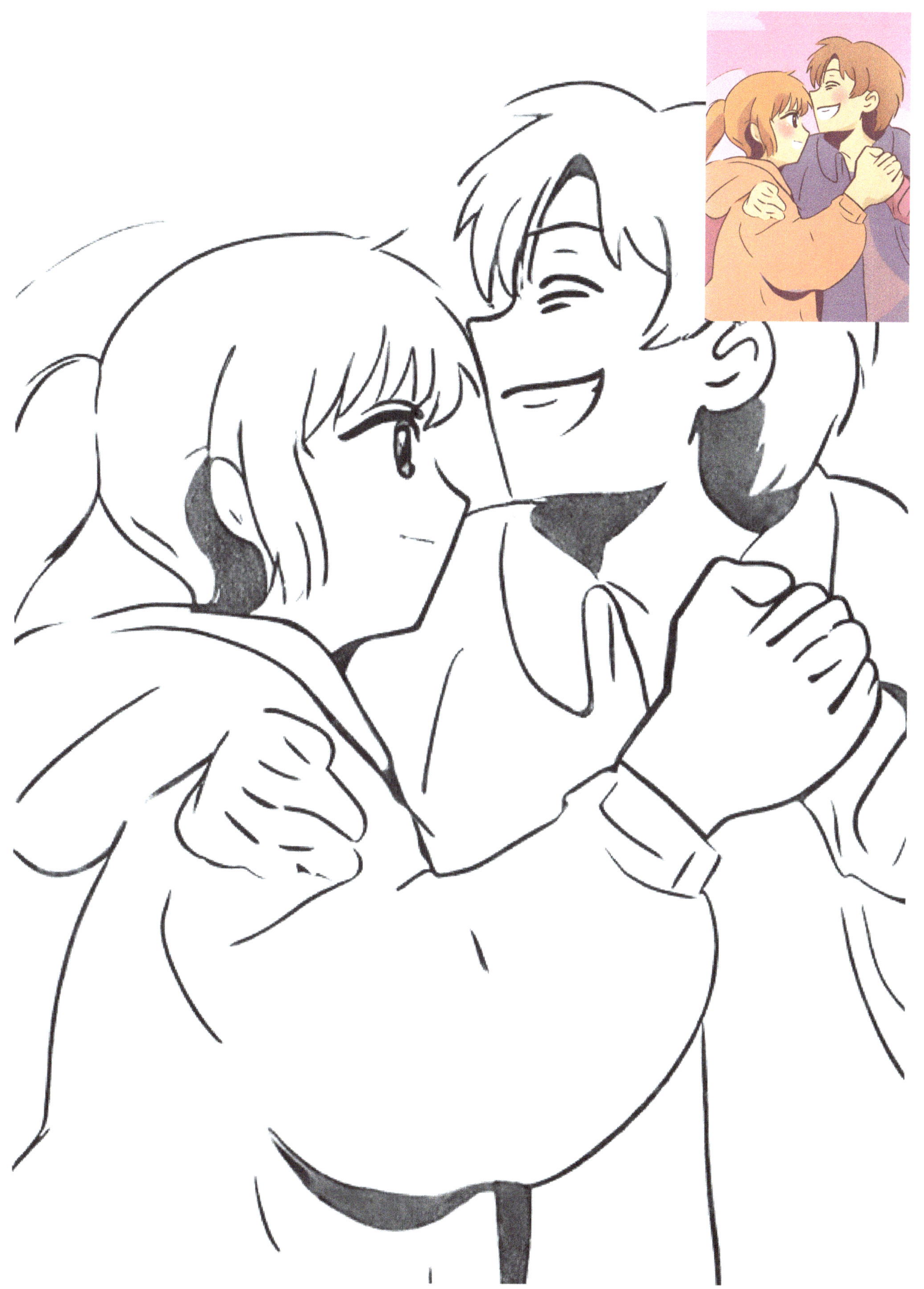

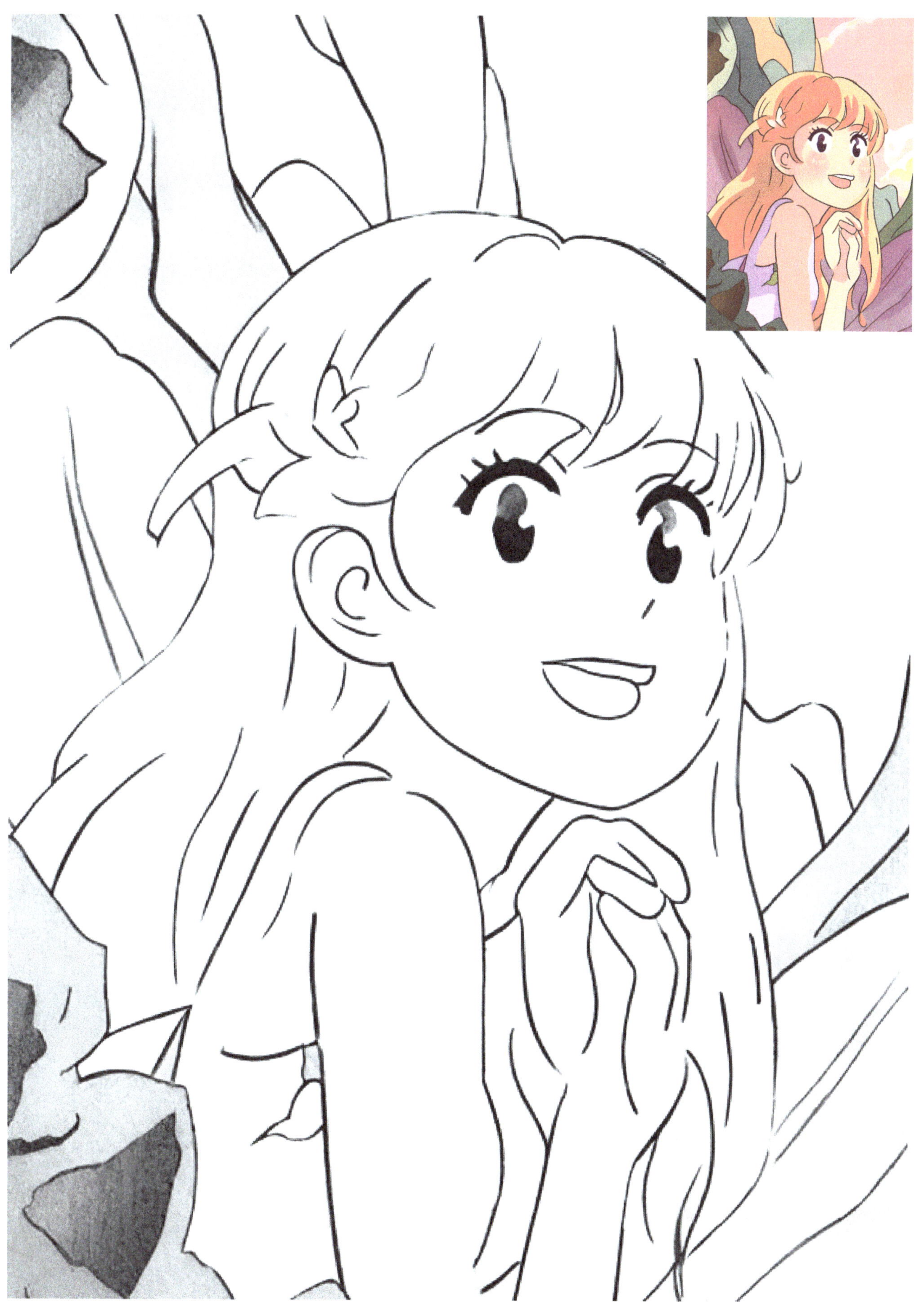

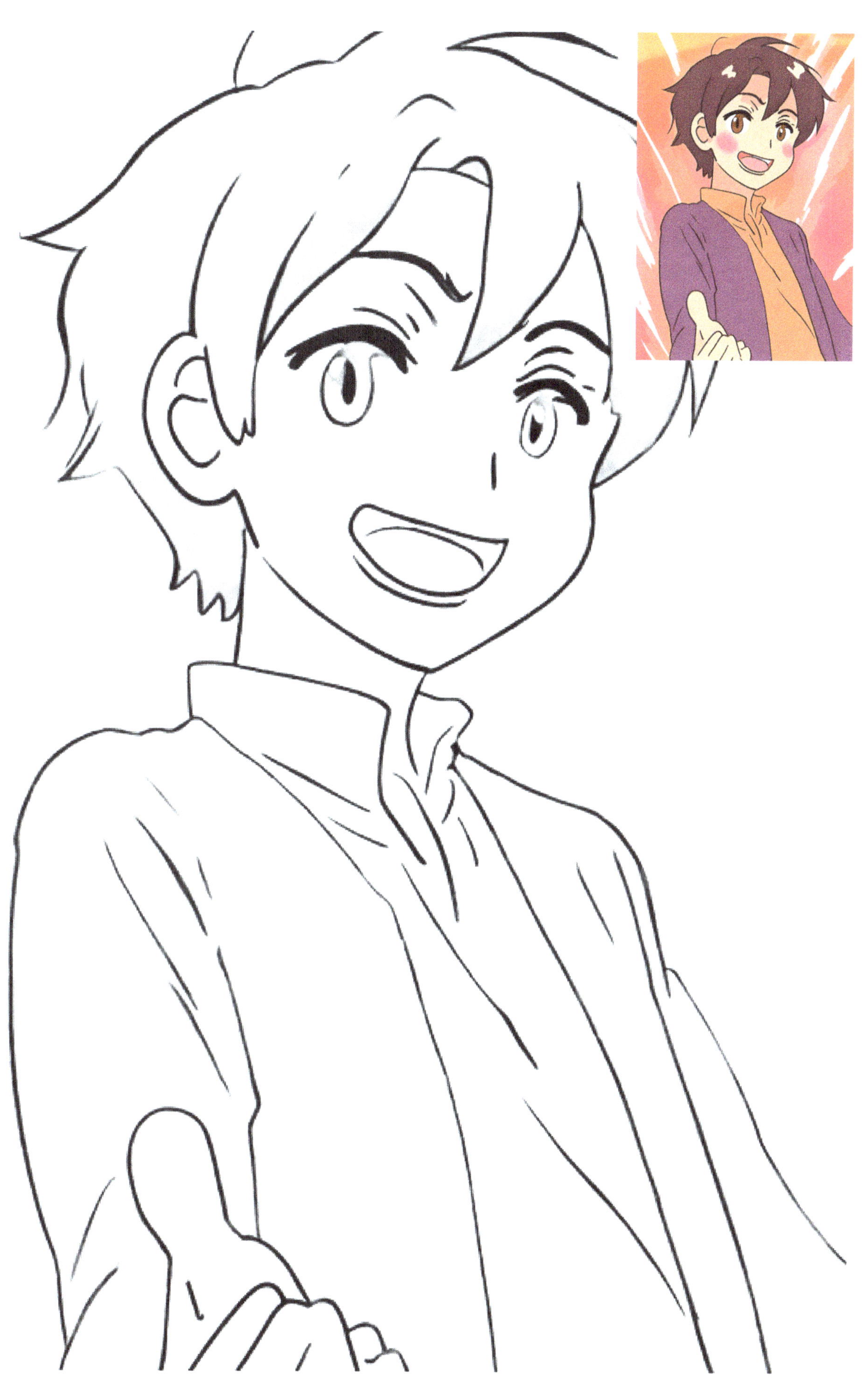

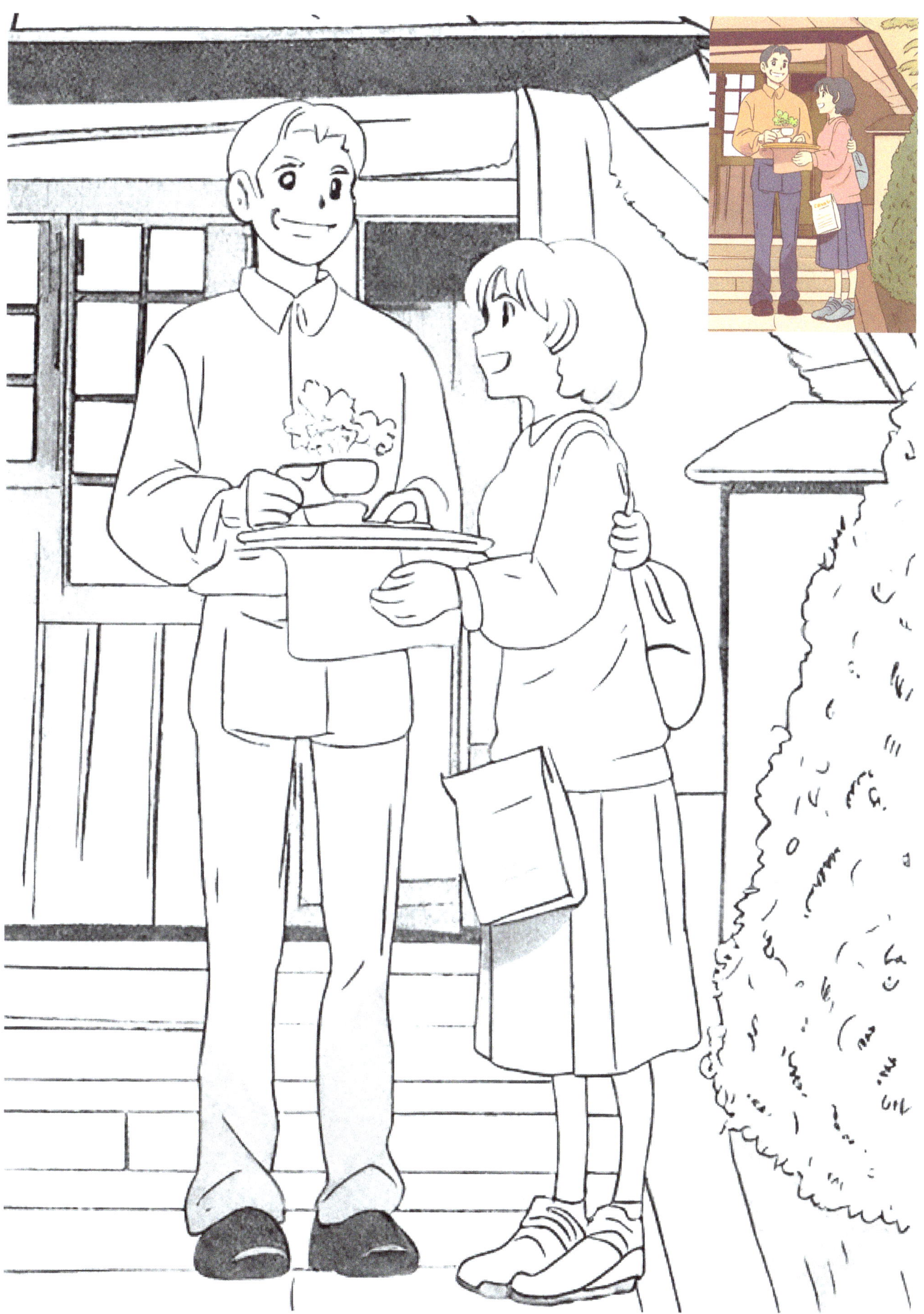

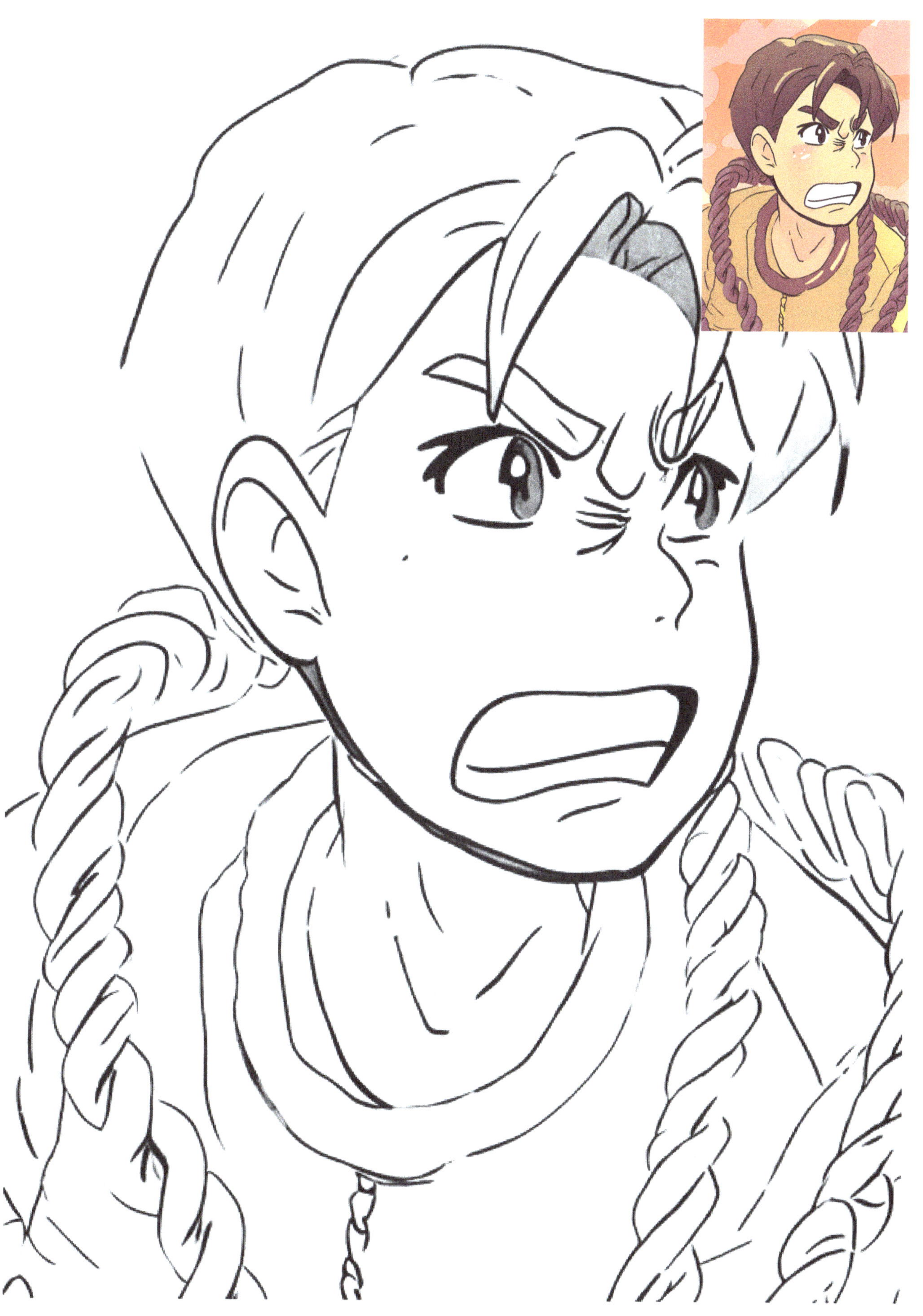